Digital Stractics

How Strategy Met Tactics and Killed the Strategic Plan

Digital Stractics

Chris Outram

Founder and Chairman, OC&C

First published 2016 by
PALGRAVE MACMILLAN

Palgrave Macmillan in the UK is an imprint of Macmillan Publishers Limited, registered in England, company number 785998, of Houndmills, Basingstoke, Hampshire RG21 6XS.

Palgrave Macmillan in the US is a division of St Martin's Press LLC, 175 Fifth Avenue, New York, NY 10010.

Palgrave Macmillan is the global academic imprint of the above companies and has companies and representatives throughout the world.

Palgrave® and Macmillan® are registered trademarks in the United States, the United Kingdom, Europe and other countries.

ISBN 978–1–137–57481–7

This book is printed on paper suitable for recycling and made from fully managed and sustained forest sources. Logging, pulping and manufacturing processes are expected to conform to the environmental regulations of the country of origin.

A catalogue record for this book is available from the British Library.

A catalog record for this book is available from the Library of Congress.

Typeset by MPS Limited, Chennai, India.

Contents

10   The Future of Stractics / 123

List of Figures and Tables

Figures

Tables

Preface and Summary

I had originally thought that the writing of my first book, *Making Your Strategy Work*, would purge me of the idea of ever writing another book. While I enjoyed writing the book, I had remarkably little desire to repeat the experience.

You can imagine my surprise therefore when six months ago, I thought back to some of the interviews for the original book which we had done with online-only (i.e. pure play) companies on the west coast of America, and it occurred to me that there was much more to say on the topic of strategy for companies in the digital world.

While most traditional companies adopt a strategic framework in which they consider their options in a three- to five-year timescale, pure plays give the impression of having little interest in undertaking the comprehensive and rigorous strategic processes which are commonplace in most of the world's medium to large corporations. While many pure plays have dreams of world domination in the form of their vision/mission statement, few of them can produce conventional strategy documents telling you how they are going to get from here to there!

Indeed, many of them exult in the fact that their planning horizons are measured in months, if not weeks or even days. The empirical process of learning by doing substitutes in large measure for the traditional strategy process.

In this sense, strategy meets tactics on the battlefield of online commerce. It is little wonder therefore that we have chosen to call this book *Digital Stractics – How Strategy Met Tactics and Killed the Strategic Plan*.

In conversations with my partners, and in particular with Anita Balchandani, the leader of OC&C's Retail practice in the UK, it was clear that many of us had experience of working with pure plays as well as hybrids (traditional companies who have had to adopt e-commerce as an essential part of their consumer proposition), but we had never taken the time to codify our views about how strategies are best developed as the world continues to digitize.

Anita and I decided that this was a very important topic in terms of trying to get under the skin of how both pure plays and hybrids have wrestled to the ground the issue of online propositions, business models, and competition. Therefore, in this book, which focuses on the issue of the fusing of strategy and tactics in a digital world, we have penned what I hope is a useful contribution to the field of strategy. Anita has been an invaluable collaborator. While I take full responsibility for what has been written, almost none of it would have been written without her encouragement, challenge, and insight.

Once again, this book does not only rely on the inputs of the OC&C partnership alone. We also thought it would be informative to go out and seek the experience and insights of some 80 entrepreneurs, CEOs, and chairmen of both pure plays and hybrids.

In this version we have focused primarily on B2C businesses such as retail, media, fast moving consumer goods, leisure and their interface with consumers. Readers from more industrial businesses should not be frustrated as they can observe, with relief, that they are not exposed to the rapidly changing challenges inherent in consumer oriented businesses. This book does not address the profound shifts that are taking place in many of these sectors due to geopolitical and technological developments that are specific to these industries. Nonetheless, we hope that the book offers some useful food for thought in terms of how the digital landscape is changing and what that means for businesses which have digital interfaces with their customers.

Strategy in the Digital World is a complex and often dynamically evolving concept. However, there do seem to be some frameworks within which both pure plays and hybrids might like to think about their strategy and business models. Most importantly, timescales collapse and Strategy and Tactics begin to blend. Indeed, we will argue that Strategy has become largely empirical in businesses with a high customer-oriented digital component. Often Strategy and Tactics have merged, and the world of STRACTICS is upon us.

It is by no means clear that either model, pure play or hybrid, is inherently advantaged over the other. Success is often industry sector-dependent. Indeed, even the phrase "pure plays" may be misleading given that, for example, while the consumer interface might very well be online and digital, there is often a very traditional back-office managing customer service and product sourcing/warehouse delivery. Indeed, one of our conclusions is that even the distinction between pure play and hybrid is increasingly redundant as more holistic business models begin to emerge.

As always, therefore, the answer to the question "Who will win?" is … It all depends!

The outputs of our deliberations and interviews are presented here for your consideration.

We hope you enjoy the book, which we summarize below:

Chapter 1   Why Traditional Strategy Does Not Work Anymore

Faced with the challenges of the increasingly fast-moving digital world, companies are no longer able to take the time to reflect on and execute traditional strategy. Hence **Stractics** – where tactics and strategy fuse as companies are forced to reassess how to win – at pace.

These changes to the landscape have resulted in fundamental changes in consumer purchasing behavior, their interaction with brands and the costs and models of doing business.

Consumers are adopting technology at an astonishing rate both within and across markets. As such, companies need to respond to the more direct interaction with consumers and react accordingly. Expectations are also increasing as a result; consumers want to be able to interact with businesses seamlessly in multiple ways, whether that is across different devices or between online and physical stores i.e. multichannel access. All these interactions mean a huge quantity of additional data is available allowing companies to gain insight into consumers and their behavior like never before. But along with this avalanche of information comes the need to respond to it rapidly and single-mindedly. Simultaneously, entrepreneurs are harnessing this data and using it to enter a market space quickly and with new high impact and often low cost models, increasing competitive intensity within and between sectors.

In response to this, the business landscape has had to evolve rapidly, with the emergence of different digital models including the emergence of complementary channels, the creation of disruptive business models, the re-segmentation of the market and even the creation of entirely new markets. The overarching bedrock of these new business models is the increase in consumer-centricity. Consumers are quick to respond and very happy to adapt to any new model which improves their experience.

New pure-plays are able to enter the market and compete, while traditional hybrid models are forced to adapt and reinvent themselves. This results in a rapidly changing industry landscape with respect to:

- new norms of measuring shareholder value
- new ways of competing
- requirements for new competencies (often in short-supply)
- new giants in the form of 'contested monopolies' and
- accelerated access to new international markets.

This speed and magnitude of change creates fertile ground for entrepreneurs who are able to adapt at a sufficiently quick pace.

The digital revolution is here to stay and traditional companies need to reinvent their approach i.e. retaining their vision whilst increasing their pace of decision making in a combination of strategy and tactics – 'Stractics'.

Chapter 2   Everything Needs to Change – or Does It?

Does this seismic change in the way companies do business and the collapse of traditional strategy into Stractics mean that all traditional learnings go out the window? This chapter takes us through each of these 'laws of gravity' in turn and argues that the answer is in fact no, the fundamental characteristics of successful businesses hold whether in the conventional or 'new' world.

Knowing your 'endgame', being clear on your competitive advantage, holding high relative market share, accessing the right capabilities and skills, understanding barriers to entry/exit and being clear on how the business makes money all continue to underpin success in this faster moving environment.

Failure to recognize these fundamentals resulted in the over-valuation and eventual demise of many businesses during the dot-com era and may continue to threaten even apparently successful digital businesses who have not yet matured fully in this new world.

Chapter 3   New Business Models for the New World: Stractics in Practice

Digital propositions and business models are largely more intuitive, faster, more accessible and more cost effective than traditional models.

It is therefore not surprising that a large number of new business models have emerged.

They can be grouped into four types:

- **Complementary/enhancement models** use digital to build on the existing proposition either through engaging consumers online or enhancing the proposition by offering a much wider range than available offline.
- **Resegmentation** by redeploying the existing business model to take advantage of lower cost of distribution and increased access to

data: new segments of the market can be accessed that may not have been cost-effective traditionally. This is particularly relevant to accessing international markets: retailers can now enter new geographies quickly and with low capital investment.

- **Disruptive models** tackle existing sectors from a new angle which can substitute either partially or wholly for traditional models using fundamentally different cost structures which enable the new entrant to massively undercut existing pricing and/or massively improve the product offering/customer experience.
- **'New New' models** which simply could not exist outside the digital sphere and which have created their own marketplaces. These marketplaces derive from entirely new ways of accessing, communicating with and interacting with consumers. Typically they can create huge communities which will present huge monetization opportunities once they mature.

Chapter 4   Pure Plays and How They Change the World

The scale and pace of online/digital development has been phenomenal.

This massive transformation has been largely led by pure plays taking advantage of low barriers to entry (low capital investment, easy to target customer bases) and being agile enough to serve high-value customers cost effectively and at high service levels.

The focus of pure plays in the short-term has been growth rather than the more traditional measures of financial success such as margins, profitability and return on capital. More particularly, they have focused on gaining a level of market share which makes subsequent market entry substantially more difficult for new entrants. Only then do they turn their attention to monetizing the model, by which stage it is very hard for traditional hybrids to compete.

Many of these pure plays are led by young, ambitious leaders with bold visions and an often obsessive passion for delivering customer satisfaction.

They benefit from high levels of direct customer feedback both in terms of the delivery of their product/service or within the product development process.

Such companies are very effective in allowing customers to drive change.

Pure plays also tend to favor speed over perfection, focusing on shaping the future over exploiting the present. This gives rise to two new sources of competitive advantage: speed and culture. Indeed, the pure play represents a new 'breed' of competitor: bold and creative, visionary, with a sense of urgency coupled with focus and flexibility, a willingness to try and fail, while focusing on (particularly consumer-facing) technology and fostering a culture which encourages all of the above.

While pure plays have led the rise of **Stractics** with their ability to operate at a rapid pace, they also have their own challenges. Such rapid rates of change mean that leaders need to take more direct control, manage risk and make decisions more rapidly and frequently. Scaling up can also be challenging as it is difficult to migrate in leadership terms from start-up to small-company to mid-cap to large operator.

Pure plays also need to plot a clear path to financial success which can be at odds with the early stage philosophies of rapid growth and increases in market share at any cost.

Chapter 5   Hybrid Players – Waking up to the New Digital Reality!

One consequence of the digital age is that barriers to entry have been lowered presumably favoring pure plays – so can Hybrids realistically compete?

"Yes" is the answer as long as they conclude that "doing nothing" is not an option. All too often Hybrids fall into the trap of either overemphasizing the value of their current business model or undervaluing their true competitive assets which is seldom the business model itself. Hybrids should embrace new business models and use their assets to make sure they Win in the new world. They should embrace cannibalization as part and parcel of winning in the digital world.

The digital marketplace requires undivided focus on (if not obsession with) consumer needs and the way consumers react to fast changing propositions, rather than the traditional focus on the size and construct of the market opportunity.

This can be a fundamental change for hybrids in terms of the way of thinking about opportunities and threats. As a response to the fast moving environment, hybrids need to start thinking early about the way in which they harness consumer insights and translate them into goals for the company, experimenting and adjusting as necessary.

Strategy is now about designing models which have the ability to adapt to consumers' changing needs and behaviors. This may not be possible where disruptive pure play models have already gained too much ground.

Hybrids must move early and decisively.

In order to compete effectively, hybrids need to establish a level playing field with pure plays in terms of talent, culture and experimentation. In turn this requires rethinking of the organization and unwinding some of the traditional business myths and organizational hierarchies. Other key changes may involve building in-house technology capabilities, changing the way investment decisions are made and adapting governance structures.

Above all, strong leadership is crucial in driving digital strategy as big cultural and business model shifts have to be made …. and quickly. An informed and single-minded leadership is critical – without it, hybrids are probably destined to watch their core businesses be progressively undermined.

Chapter 6   Pure Plays versus Hybrids – A Fight to the Finish?

There are a number of factors that will determine whether a market is susceptible to digital disruption:

- Can the product can be digitized?
- Are consumers unhappy with existing offerings (too slow, inconvenient, uneconomic, etc.)?
- Can digitization undercut the traditional cost model?

Who will win then comes down to more traditional fundamentals of strategy: market demand, proposition design, fundamentals of economical supply, competition, etc.

Even in sectors where digital will be critical, hybrid companies still have three secret weapons: brand, buying scale and supply chain. But are hybrid companies visionary enough to recognize the potential of digital whilst harnessing their existing advantages?

Digital opportunities do not necessarily mandate a full-scale overhaul but may take the form of new digital products or services, digital transactions or selling a subset of products through new online channels. The question is often whether the hybrid can move fast enough to prevent the rug being pulled from under their feet by fleet of foot pure plays.

This chapter also looks at some key examples of digital disruption in some unlikely fields including legal services and banking.

In some sectors hybrids can hold their own, particularly where there is low purchase frequency, high purchase price/risk, or complex technical decisions in the buying process – at least for the time being.

While there is frequently a place for both hybrid and pure play models in many sectors, the line between the two will become increasingly blurred as companies migrate towards the optimal digital/physical business model.

Chapter 7   The Principles Underpinning Success in the World of Stractics

The key insights that have emerged through the course of the book to this point, can be summarized in ten principles of equal relevance to both hybrids and pure plays alike. And which will prevent both pure plays and hybrids from falling victim to some of the most obvious pitfalls of the digital world of Stractics.

1. Vision and purpose should create a sense of ambition and direction in the organization.
2. Consumers are central and should be obsessed about from their acquisition, through to driving high levels of customer service and retention. Data is key in this battle.
3. Embeding the right planning horizons is a critical part of instilling agility and flexibility into the organization– no longer is the 5 year plan relevant, and even a one-year plan needs to be frequently reviewed and revised, along with the associated budgets.
4. Investing in competitive advantage remains critical, whether it is the business model, the proposition itself or an efficient supply chain. Innovation is at the core of organizations in the digital world.
5. Harnessing technology effectively, particularly when it is at the front-end, consumer-focused part of the business cannot be underestimated. The cost of poor technology is high and the speed at which companies need to move in order to stay cutting edge can be breath-taking.
6. Building a robust and integrated business model incorporating staff, suppliers and consumers and involving all in the creation and delivery of the proposition is a key source of differentiation.
7. Setting high standards in quality of people and the culture in which they work is required to effectively implement Stractics.
8. Constantly reinventing yourself needs to include the concept of effectively 'disrupting yourself'. The status quo is almost always out of date in the digital world.
9. Implementing a new governance model will ease the implementation of the new cultural norms required to compete effectively in the digital world.
10. Building a fit-for-purpose organization with appropriate processes, and an agile culture must be contemplated.

These principles apply to both pure plays and hybrids but whilst pure plays will probably adopt many of them naturally, hybrids need to adhere to them however uncomfortable they might feel.

Chapter 8   Strategy Processes in the World of Stractics

Given the speed of change in the digital world, strategy has transformed from a linear process to a highly interactive process operating in the context of vision, tactics and finance, collectively known as Stractics.

Nevertheless, businesses must still incorporate many of the fundamental laws of gravity of good strategy. These include rendering a vision as to how the business fits into the world, defining where money is to be made, developing a business model tactically, planning growth and how you will scale up, not to mention how you will ultimately crystallize value for shareholders.

To adapt to the technologically-intensive and customer-obsessed digital world, businesses can pursue a four-step process.

- Step 1 involves establishing an ambitious but achievable vision.
- Step 2 involves establishing 90-day strategic goals for every team in the organization, and also recalibrating these goals every 90 days.
- Step 3 requires a regular refresh of the annual financial plans.
- Step 4 entails installing new metrics/KPIs so that the success of the strategy can be monitored.

As a critical part of these steps, businesses must focus on people and customer technology (CT, not just IT). On the people side, a clear organizational purpose, emphasis on talent, and inspiring leadership are key ingredients for success, whilst in terms of technology, the company's approach needs to be reconfigured frequently and dynamically.

Chapter 9   Advice from the Top: Stractical Tips from Our Digital CEOs

Top Stractics tips for pure plays and hybrids differ significantly due to the nature of their starting points. Whilst pure plays may find it easier to adapt to the world of Stractics than their hybrid counterparts, senior business leaders have offered tailored tips to both types of businesses.

For pure plays, CEOs have advised prioritizing the creation of a suitably compelling vision and the implied ambition. The next priority is to focus on talent, structure and finance/risk. Consumer generated feedback should be used frequently to iterate propositions quickly and frequently. Market share should be the focus rather than just revenue growth, whilst monetization options should be thought through early on. Corporate culture should be friendly/collaborative and technology should be invested in to build world-class competence. Leadership is of key importance but should be changed at the correct inflection point of the business as it moves from a founder lead business to a more professionalized business.

Hybrid CEOs have emphasized the importance of employing leaders with vision about the role of digital. These CEO's discourage the use of the word "cannibalization" in order to move away from the mindset of doing damage to the existing business. They also recommend seizing early mover advantages relentlessly. Nimble and joined up organizational structures should be established early on, although digital capability may be built, at least initially, as a separate unit. More generally, classical heads of IT should not be pushed into taking charge of digital technology – the "geeks" should be empowered via an appropriate environment, and then incentivized via correctly aligned KPIs. Operationally, hybrids should also consider committing fully to a series of relatively near-term digital goals, tolerating ambiguity and even failure, not to mention creating a fast-paced, a yet agile environment.

Chapter 10   The Future of Stractics

In theory, pure plays and hybrids are differentiated by the fact that the latter owns legacy assets. However, this distinction becomes rather blurred in the real world. Pure play businesses are use both digital and physical attributes to optimize their values and strategies. Online retailer's product storage and delivery often mirror those of a hybrid retailer.

In in this fast-moving environment, "digital" will soon cease to be a useful term to describe the old or the new world as hybrids and pure plays converge given that consumer interfaces will increasingly be digital and yet the back-office may sometimes remain entirely physical.

However for pure plays and hybrids alike, the key preoccupation must be to remain obsessed by one's own customers and their "journey". Organizations must keep on top of technology as it alters the consumer's interest levels and behaviors. Businesses need to rethink organizational, cultural and talent acquisition strategies to operate successfully in the digital world. Lastly, all must ensure that the leadership of the company buys into the concept (and the reality) of the new world, treating digital as an opportunity rather than a threat.

In short, Stractics will eventually become fully integrated into core business models. In response, planning cycles will collapse from the three- to five-year strategic plan to a position backed up with a much more empirical process of planning often rooted in 90 to 360 day cycles.

When this happens, the three-year plan will indeed be dead.

Acknowledgment

While the author welcomes and very much appreciates the input of his interviewees, he nevertheless takes full responsibility for this book and its contents.

List of Contributors

Keith Allen, Former COO, Mecom

Annet Aris, Professor, INSEAD

Nevzat Aydın, CEO, Yemeksepeti

Eduardo Baek, COO and Founder, eÓtica

Sachin Bansal, CEO, Flipkart

Ilker Baydar, CEO, Markafoni

Jan Bayer, President, BILD and WELT Group

Desirée Bollier, Chief Executive, Value Retail PLC

Toon Bouten, CEO, Tomorrow Focus AG

Matt Brittin, VP Northern and Central Europe, Google

Mark Britton, Founder and CEO, AVVO

Jerry Buhlmann, CEO, Aegis

Brian Cassin, CEO, Experian

Patrick Cescau, Non-Executive Chairman, InterContinental Hotels Group Plc

Andrew Crawley, Chief Commercial Officer, British Airways

Mike Darcey, CEO, News UK

Asmita Dubey, Chief Marketing Officer, L'Oreal China

Emre Ekmekçi, Head of Business Development, Hepsiburada

Vitor Falleiros, Head of Planning, Dafiti

Jonathan Feroze, Co-Founder, BMI Research

Jonathan Gabbai, Head of International Mobile Product, eBay

Krishan Ganesh, Founder, Portea Medical

Jean-Christophe Garbino, CEO, Kiabi

Marc van Gelder, Former CEO, Peapod and Mediq

Derk Haank, CEO, Springer Science+Business Media

Rick Hamada, CEO, Avnet

Michael E. Hansen, CEO, Cengage Learning

Barney Harford, CEO and Director, Orbitz Worldwide

Florian Heinemann, Co-Founder and Managing Director, Project A

Rainer Hillebrand, Vice Chairman of Executive Board, Otto Group

Robert Hohman, CEO, Glassdoor

Jeffrey R. Holzschuh, Chairman, Morgan Stanley

Mark Hunter, CEO, Molson Coors Brewing Company

Sebastian James, Group CEO, Dixons Carphone

Jørgen Vig Knudstorp, CEO and President, LEGO Group

Alexander Kudlich, Group Managing Director, Rocket Internet

James A. Lawrence, Former Chairman, Rothschild North America

Richard Londesborough, Co-Founder, BMI Research

Guilherme Loureiro, CEO, Walmart Brazil

Dan Mallin, Managing Partner, Magnet 360

Paul Manduca, Chairman, Prudential

Anna Manz, Group Strategy Director, Diageo plc

Luis Maroto, President and CEO, Amadeus

James Meekings, Founder, Funding Circle

Brian Newman, Global Head of e-Commerce, PepsiCo

Mark Newton-Jones, CEO, Mothercare

Frederik Nieuwenhuys, Founder / Entrepreneur, Multiple businesses

Roger Parry, Chairman, YouGov

Gavin Patterson, Chief Executive, BT Group Plc

Elsa Pekmez Atan, EVP, Enpara

Richard Pennycook, CEO, The Co-operative Group

Robert Philpott, CEO, Harte Hanks

Marcelo Picanço, CFO, Porto Seguro

Peter Plumb, CEO, MoneySuperMarket.com

Michael Polk, President and CEO, Newell Rubbermaid

Spencer Rascoff, CEO, Zillow

John Roberts, CEO, AO

Sidar Sahin, CEO, Peak Games

Antoine de Saint-Affrique, Former President of Foods, Unilever, now CEO of Barry Callebaut

Marjorie Scardino, Chairman, The MacArthur Foundation

Cassius Schymura, Director of Cards and Personal Banking Products, Santander

Tom Seery, Founder and CEO, RealSelf

S. Sivakumar, Divisional Chief Executive of the Agri Business Division, ITC Agribusiness

Artur Smolarek, Managing Director, Health Insurance, PZU Group

Sir Martin Sorrell, Group CEO, WPP

Kurt Staelens, CEO, Macintosh

Tim Steiner, CEO, Ocado

Andy Street, Managing Director, The John Lewis Partnership

Rogério Takayanagi, CEO, TIM Fiber

Prashant Tandon, Managing Director and Co-Founder, HealthKart.com

Anne Tse, General Manager, New Business, Greater China, PepsiCo

John Walden, Group CEO, Home Retail Group

Mike Walsh, CEO, LexisNexis

Christian Wegner, Board Member, ProSiebenSat.1

Stefan Winners, Board Member, Burda Digital Holdings

Gang Yu, Chairman and Co-Founder, Yihaodian

Introduction

Is the classic strategic plan really dead?

If the sector in which you are competing is deeply involved in the digital world then the answer is probably "Yes." And that is what we will argue in this book.

In terms of pure plays (companies who started their lives as pure digital businesses), they very seldom write a strategic plan. It is not certain they even know what one is. Yes, they have a vision, but after that, their planning horizons seldom go further than three months or, at most, a year.

As you can imagine, hybrids (companies who traditionally enjoyed a business not challenged by the Internet) have been weaned onto three-year planning cycles for many decades. Despite what is written in their plans, they often unexpectedly have to contemplate joining in battle with pure plays, as their consumers wish to browse and purchase products online. Whether for organizational or cultural reasons, they often have many challenges and problems as they fire up their digital bazookas and tanks.

But let's start at the beginning.

There are some immutable truths which relate to all businesses both online and offline.

Whether you are a pure play or a hybrid, you have to pay attention to a number of principles – and not one of them, but all of them – if you wish to have a successful business:

• You need an ambitious Vision or End-game;
• You have to have competitive differentiation/advantage;
• You need to strive for high relative market share;
• You have to establish/protect barriers to entry;
• You must know how your model will make money;
• … And you must have access to the right skills/capabilities.

While pure plays have the benefit of a visionary (if not apocalyptic) mission, they usually score well on all of the above except perhaps the fifth, relating to having a clear sense of how they will monetize their concepts. But as a counter-weight, they also enjoy other powerful advantages:

• Investors seem to be stampeding to give them money at any price if the vision is bold enough;
• Their leadership is usually young and motivating;
• They attract very talented technologists and marketing people who are incredibly dedicated, loyal, and committed, and are not necessarily there for the money;
• They are on top of (consumer-orientated) technology;
• They create agile, flexible, informal, and fun cultures;
• They are energetic and committed;
• They work at pace;
• They experiment and tolerate a degree of failure as part of the journey.

…. So even when their model is ultimately found to be flawed (think Boo.com) and is ultimately caught out because it fails to make money, they can be very disruptive to markets to the cost of other pure plays and hybrids alike.

Indeed, when you stand back from what is happening, pure plays are bringing a number of game-changing capabilities into play:

- Making the complex easy-to-use;
- Working at speed;
- Making propositions available at any time and at any place;
- Benefiting from new world economics which tend to be capital-light.

In turn, this has seen four new business models come to the fore;

- Complementary channels based upon improved consumer engagement, multichannel shopping;
- Extension of the existing business model by expanding market reach through the re-segmentation of the market or geographic expansion;
- Market disruption by simultaneously and massively improving customer benefits at lower cost, e.g. Uber;
- New/new markets which offer consumers entirely new propositions never even contemplated before, e.g. Twitter.

In the face of this digital onslaught, hybrids really struggle to adjust their business models, which are often ill-suited to attracting those game-changing individuals who will push the digital boundaries forward. Such people are young and ambitious, prefer informal rather than rigid cultures, enjoy autonomy and creativity, and do not adapt well to the more rigid cultures of established businesses.

Such people also need to be managed according to a slightly different set of rules which are alien to most traditional cultures where cannibalization is frowned upon, experimentation discouraged, and failure punished, not tolerated. Typically, '(information) technology' is applied to big, inflexible, back-office systems rather than the fleet-of-foot, often-changing consumer-oriented digital application software. Switching from a "systems" to "software" culture is non-trivial. We are moving from an information technology world to a customer technology world.

So in the face of these powerful advantages that pure plays appear to enjoy and the disadvantages that hybrids have to endure, should the latter just give up?

No – hybrids have a different set of powerful competitive weapons to deploy in the digital wars.

The power of brands should never be underestimated. They bring with them substantial customer bases, which are often loyal and which will give the brands a chance to catch up. The existence of a substantial "real" business brings with it purchasing power/scale, and often the support of suppliers, who find the new digital world almost as intimidating and uncertain as hybrids do.

At the very least these assets allow hybrids the time to regroup and get behind a new digital business model. However, this time window is measured in the six to 12 month period not in a three- to four-year digital holiday. There remains an imperative to act and to act sooner rather than later given that consumer behavior is moving rapidly, having been stimulated by the digital onslaught of new applications, propositions, and business models.

For hybrids to have a chance of success they have to move at speed to embrace ten success factors. They do not guarantee success, but they do provide the minimum conditions for waging battle with the digital insurgents.

1. **Get leaders with vision**. If the battle is not masterminded from the board room it is very unlikely that the necessary resources will be deployed to "arm" the armies of hybrids in an appropriate fashion.
2. **Outlaw the word "cannibalization."** The old adage that if you do not do it to yourself then someone else will do it to you remains as true as ever. It is only a matter of time before the new models will encroach on the traditional frameworks which made your company so successful and which are now increasingly redundant.
3. **No dabbling**. Do not make the mistake of undertaking this journey in a risk-avoidance and half-hearted way. That is not the route to success when your competitors seem to have unlimited financial and people resources.
4. **Align the organization from top to bottom**. Tissue rejection is all too easy if all levels in the organization have not been sensitized (and

possibly even incentivized) to the need of succeeding in the digital world, and puts long-term futures at risk.

5. **Align online and offline sales key performance indicators (KPIs)**. People tend to behave according to the way they are measured and rewarded (both financially and in terms of esteem). If you continue to measure performance in "old world ways," then whatever new resources you have managed to attract into the company to wage the digital battle with you will soon be depleted.

6. **Do not put your IT head in charge**. Empower the Geeks: the ways you attract and manage human resources best able to wage the digital battles is critical. In addition "leopards do not change their spots;" executives who have been trained to manage large multi-year systems projects will not be able to deploy resources optimally when the cycles of invent, deploy, review, renew are measured in weeks rather than years. This is about customer technology, not information technology.

7. **Accept digital as an opportunity not a threat**. In many businesses, it is entirely possible that the revenues and profits available in the digital world are only a fraction of those that were originally enjoyed in the traditional. No matter; you have no choice but to go there, as the alternative is to have no business at all.

8. **Reward experimentation and tolerate (some) failure**. With technology cycles moving apace and consumer behavior changing rapidly as a result of many different information and entertainment opportunities, there is a huge payoff from having many experiments parallel-tracking simultaneously. There is no time to have a sequential approach to product-/proposition-development in the digital world. You have to let many hares start running and then back those that are leading the pack.

9. **Adopt 90-day planning cycles ... and budgets to match**. The accessibility of technology and the ability to get very rapid and frequent feedback about your experiments means that you need to adopt relatively short planning cycles that allow you to experiment and then back the successes – 90 days is typical. Budgeting therefore becomes a much less precise art and is directional rather than specific. A very uncomfortable feeling for most hybrids, who historically have been able to plan three years ahead with relative certainty, not to mention impunity!

10. **Obsess about the consumer**. Historically, market research would tell you a great deal about your customers, and you could therefore plan activity many years in advance. In the digital world, this luxury is no longer available. Consumers are increasingly technologically savvy, get information extraordinarily quickly – including peer-group ratings of what works and what does not work, and hence are able to change behavior incredibly rapidly. If you are not obsessing about your consumers and the way they are "behaving today" then you are highly likely to lose the digital war.

In the last chapter of this book you will find an admirable example of a hybrid who did all of the above and is now a very much larger business than it was before the digital age.

Nevertheless, uncertainties about technology and consumer behavior render it impossible for any digital business (pure play or hybrid) to make credible long-term plans. It is possible (and probably essential) to have a vision and an intent about what you are trying to achieve commercially. You may even be able to put an outline financial plan together which sets out the direction of travel. But to go further than this and to attempt to hypothesize with any degree of certainty (and possibly even confidence) exactly what your products/propositions are likely to be in three years' time is probably folly in the digital world.

Investors, boards and even senior management of hybrids are not yet universally comfortable with the uncertainties implied by the digital era. The pure plays who are changing the rules of the game therefore do have a window of opportunity to steal share while hybrids adjust to the new world. On the other hand, those hybrids lucky enough to have an enlightened senior management should be able to move rapidly both to protect their traditional business and then to extend into new channels/geographies/propositions so that they win not only the immediate battle but also the overall war.

Whatever the outcome, it is probably not in line with whatever strategic plan they might have written a few years ago.

The strategic plan may indeed be dead.

chapter 1

Why Traditional Strategy Does Not Work Anymore!

Traditional strategy processes require time as well as thoughtful analysis about consumers, markets, competitors, and the detailed workings of business models, as well as a deep understanding of industry/player economics.

Once this broad range of insight is assembled, companies go through a complex process in order to make sure that they have sufficient consensus to debate and conclude around a winning, straightforward, and compelling – not to mention sustainable – strategy.

The ability to execute such processes does not exist in the digital world, where things move fast, technology evolution can spring surprises upon the unwary, competitors are non-obvious and information about them is sparse and ephemeral.

"Three-year plans are indeed giving way to Stractics!"

Marc van Gelder, former CEO of Peapod, the world's first online grocer, originally founded in the US and ultimately bought by Ahold in 2000, and Mediq, the leading Dutch pharmaceutical wholesaler, said,

> Although it took longer to get going than originally predicted the Internet revolution has fulfilled all its early promises. We are still in the very beginning of this revolution which will have major impact on

traditional players in many sectors like Retail, Banking, Insurance – and it will impact large FMCG players as well as traditional wholesalers. Social media are only just beginning to affect traditional players.

"The world is different now," observed Andy Street, MD of the John Lewis Partnership, one of the UK's leading department stores. "You just have to pay attention – the world is speeding up in the digital era." A senior executive of one of the world's largest pure plays concurs: "The imperatives in the digital world are very simple – execute faster, cheaper, and better."

But just how different is that world today?

We believe that there are some fundamental and irreversible shifts in the world which require companies to re-examine how they compete and win. They are:

- Consumer adoption of technology
- Channel proliferation
- Technology and data explosion
- Competitive dynamism

These changes of behavior belie even more fundamental shifts in the cost of doing business which are heralded by the digital age. Costs are lowered in many parts of the cost structure:

- Cost of search/access which allow customers and suppliers to find each other
- Cost of transactions (ordering and paying)
- Cost of innovation (and its speed)

Consumers have adapted to the digital era at a speed which could not have been contemplated a decade ago. As Professor Aris of INSEAD Business School said, "Adoption curves in the digital age show a very strong tipping point effect and at the same time the speed of adoption is increasing fast."

Nowhere is this phenomenon starker than when you consider the rate of growth in smartphone penetration, which has been rapid and pronounced, particularly in the emerging economies.

Figure 1.1 shows this acceleration in the pace at which consumer technologies have been "democratized" over time. The iPod, which was a successful introduction, sold circa 35 million units in the three years after its launch. The iPhone was nearly eight times more far-reaching, with circa 240 million units over the equivalent post-launch period. Only two years after the iPhone, the Android operating system has far surpassed that with nearly one billion devices sold only three years after launch.

This acceleration of technology and technology adoption has also enabled the creation of a more level playing field for consumers in different countries. The gap between the traditional digital "haves" and "have nots" is being closed. When we consider m-commerce (mobile commerce) penetration, the emerging economies now surpass many of the G7 nations as Figure 1.2 shows.

Behind this technology adoption lie fundamental shifts in consumer behavior. If you do not understand or track these shifts you will be left behind. Traditional approaches often have to be abandoned in favor of more responsive business models as evidenced by Tom

Traditional approaches often have to be abandoned

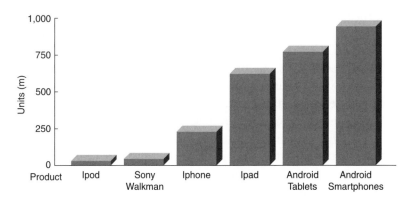

FIGURE 1.1 / Sales of key devices three years post launch

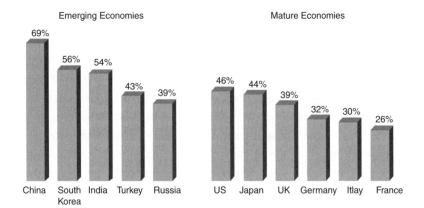

FIGURE 1.2 Emerging economies are the m-commerce leaders (percentage of smartphones used for making purchases*)
Note: *Smartphone owners who have ever used their phones to make a purchase.

Seery, CEO and Founder of RealSelf, who said, "Companies need to abandon their product roadmaps, however compelling/logical, and start listening to customer feedback which will align them with the customer journey. You should never be so arrogant to think you know more than your consumers."

Nevertheless, it is not all downsides for the traditional player, as evidenced by Michael Polk, CEO at Newell Rubbermaid, the leading US marketer of consumer products:

> The digital age should be seen as an era of entrepreneurial opportunity. It is also an era of challenge where risks need to be understood, the consequences of no-barriers-to-entry predicted, and the impact of fundamentally changed consumer behaviors/choices internalized. In other words, fast moving consumer goods companies need to understand, explore, and take advantage of their understanding of how consumers think and navigate their choices. This heralds new marketing models for brands.

In terms of channel proliferation, today's consumers are confident about digital commerce and therefore happy to interact with businesses in multiple ways. They think nothing of moving between a PC, their mobile, and a tablet, and engaging with brands via their website, Twitter and

YouTube – all in the blink of an eye. As Luis Arjona, Head of Market Expansion of eBay Brazil, commented, "People do not want to go to malls where they can only visit a few stores of a given category, when they can go online and visit hundreds."

The consumer is spoilt for choice, often being able to access both the physical manifestation of the business they wish to patronize as well as the online version, which will often offer multiple delivery options in terms both of speed of delivery and location of delivery (home or a collection point). This point was emphasized by Jean-Christophe Garbino, CEO of Kiabi, the French multichannel retailer, and raises particular challenges for multichannel businesses as they seek to "provide a customer experience which is fully integrated across all channels – it's what customers expect nowadays."

And if consumer attitudes and channel proliferation were not enough to convince you when you try to explain this phenomenon of the fundamental nature of market change, constant and rapid evolutions in technology and its ability to collect, disseminate and process huge amounts of data certainly would.

In terms of itemizing what has changed, it is difficult to know where to start. You certainly have to cover, inter alia:

- The rise in computing power
- Device proliferation
- Networking
- Internet connectivity (4G, Wi-Fi etc.)

In addition, the ability to collect and store vast amounts of data opens up the potential for a seismic shift in the possible insights into consumers and their behavior on a scale never witnessed before. Increasingly, simpler-to-use tools are being developed which allow you to query and analyze these massive databases and to draw out insights well beyond the ability of mere mortals. And we have hardly even started, given that artificial intelligence and machine learning are set to advance these capabilities even further over the next five to ten years.

The dissemination of this information through internal corporate mechanisms is dwarfed by the power of consumer-managed networks like Facebook, WhatsApp, etc. Reputations and brands can be made or destroyed within hours. Wonderful or embarrassing incidents can be experienced around the world in minutes. The Internet is truly unforgiving and must be harnessed enthusiastically, but with great care. Robert Hohman, CEO of glassdoor, a US jobs and recruiting site, gave a good example of this, "The biggest challenge recently has been the adoption of mobile and social media, meaning that connectedness on the Internet has experienced a tectonic shift. You only have to think about Uber (taxi bookings/payments) or Airbnb (bed and breakfast booking) to see how fast emergent models can become ubiquitous."

By harnessing these shifts in consumer behavior, channel options, and technological capability, it is not surprising that the more enterprising entrepreneurs and entrepreneurial companies have built new business models and attacked the more slow-moving traditional competitors and markets. They are new, agile, aggressive, and focus more on growth than profitability – a dangerous combination against which to compete if you are a traditional business.

Competitive dynamism has therefore increased dramatically, with the competitive arena shifting seismically.

The business arena has got that much more challenging, as noted by Patrick Cescau, CEO of Intercontinental Hotels Group: "One of the features of the digital era has been that new competitors have emerged. You therefore need to understand how landscapes are changing and the nature of the choices that you have to make … At pace."

Sidar Sahin of Turkey's Peak Games confirmed these new rules of the game: "To succeed you have got to read the customer feedback in real time – looking at it monthly is far too slow – that is why small, agile teams win." On the one hand, the early pioneers of the digital world, such as Amazon, have heightened the level of competitive intensity in their respective sectors. And on the other hand, new competitors have been entering in substantial numbers, occupying niches and creating new business models which could over time render numerous (but by no means all) incumbents irrelevant.

Faced with the fundamental shifts described above, it is not surprising that the business landscape has had to transform radically and rapidly. There are indeed many Internet-only, digital competitors in many industry sectors, not least retail, banking, taxis, securities trading, etc., where new business models can fundamentally undermine/ transform traditional industry folklore. The rules, structure, and even the economics of sectors can be fundamentally redefined.

In many, if not all sectors, traditional businesses have responded and created their own digital offers.

In one or two industries, however, it was too little, too late.

For instance, it is almost impossible to find a thriving "physical only" consumer-oriented Business to Consumer (B2C) travel agency nowadays. The vast majority of consumer travel bookings are now made online, whether it is flight and hotel only or complex package holidays, with the possible exception of very premium offerings with highly complex itineraries.

On the other hand, corporate travel remains in the hands of a limited number of high service level, specialist travel companies, e.g. American Express. Only limited inroads have been made by online travel specialists. (Although, of course, the corporate travel agents utilize a great number of online resources to carry out their job.)

The digital revolution has enabled a number of very different business models to emerge, where the role of the digital business varies significantly. As an example of the different digital models, we list the four most prominent below which will be elaborated in more detail in Chapter 3.

Complementary Channels

In this model, digital enables consumers to access products and propositions in ways which are entirely complementary to the traditional/

conventional business. Many retail businesses fit into this model in the sense that a significant number of consumers continue to wish to touch and feel the product, while many are quite happy to have limited interaction with the product and purchase it online. These online channels coexist happily with physical stores that demonstrate the product and allow the consumer an element of engagement not available online.

Re-segmenting the Market

Digital/online has expanded certain markets by enabling the identification of consumers/customers who were previously underserved by traditional/ conventional models. Often these models had cost structures which rendered such segments of the marketplace unprofitable or unreachable. In the UK, for example, Funding Circle has created a business based on bringing together consumers who have savings which earn very little interest with small businesses who are desperate for capital, but are unattractive to the big banks. By providing essentially an "exchange," where buyers and sellers are put into contact, the market for small business loans has been extended. Why has this model worked? Its founder, James Meekings explained: "Pure plays tend to create their own ecosystems while hybrids tend to think about the Internet merely as a distribution model."

The Disruptive Alternative

In some markets, online and digital players can entirely undermine traditional business models. Many newspapers that have undifferentiated content are at risk of being entirely dis-intermediated by online news channels. Indeed, general world news is now readily available through any number of online portals. In some cases these portals have been created by early-mover, traditional newspaper companies. For instance, the Daily Mail Online is one of the biggest news websites in the world and is accessed by a global audience. Many of its audience actually believe that the Daily Mail Online is based in their country/region, given that its newsgathering process is a 24/7 activity undertaken in journalistic centers around the world – the journalists appear never to sleep and its readers are continuously up-to-date; this is great example of a UK hybrid surviving disruption by beating the disruptors at their own game! Indeed, Mike Darcey, CEO of The Times of London, characterized the Daily Mail Online as an entirely new product: "The *Daily Mail* is a UK print product while the Mail Online is a global celebrity news service targeted at a different audience." Sidar Sahin, the founder of Peak Games in Turkey also confirmed that: "Disruption is not only about technology, it's all about changing people's way of thinking and their perspectives."

Similarly, Betfair in the UK has undermined traditional betting shops by creating an online exchange between more sophisticated/professional betting consumers, some of whom would like to place bets and some of whom would like to take bets. This is now a multibillion-dollar business.

The Creation of New Markets

Both Google and Facebook have created markets for propositions where none existed before.

The ability for Google to use emerging technologies to search huge numbers of documents rapidly has created a multibillion dollar corporation which is now diversifying rapidly into many other activities.

Facebook, on the other hand, simply (but using very sophisticated technology) puts consumers in touch with their friends and potential contacts in a way which allows them to communicate rapidly and to share experiences in a comprehensive and almost instantaneous way. Neither of these markets existed in terms of consumer propositions and yet both of them have created many hundreds of billions of dollars of value for their inventors.

The digital revolution, therefore, is changing many aspects of the commercial landscape, particularly where consumers are involved. Patrick Cescau, the CEO of Intercontinental Hotels Group, observed that

> the digital era requires you to rewrite the narrative of your company as you shift away from traditional, hard assets and focus more on brand,

customer service etc. The use of the enduring realities of the digital world where you need to make the whole organization think about how your consumer/customer thinks about your product and proposition, and where technology is at the heart of your business. The business has to become customer-centric, taking an integrated view of the customer across all the touch points that you have with them.

Consumers are surprisingly receptive to new business models and ways of behaving, particularly if these simplify their interaction with the product/proposition/service provider. Indeed consumers will abandon traditional brands, even ones with a near 100% awareness amongst households.

Consumers value these new and simple propositions so highly that new brands can be created at light-speed and with great effect ... And old brands can be undermined or, at worst, abandoned.

The power of new, simple brands was highlighted in the Siegel & Gale's Simplicity Index for 2014 in which 12,000-plus consumers globally were asked to rate conventional brands on their simplicity. Their research showed that in traditional markets, 38% of consumers are willing to pay more for simpler experiences and 70% of consumers are more likely to recommend a brand because it is simple.

When extending their research to "digital disrupter brands" like Uber, they concluded that such brands would take eight out of the top 10 places in the US if included. They reported as follows: "A new breed of [online] brands is emerging, and they're disrupting the status quo, changing consumer expectations. Though they span different industries, they possess a common characteristic – simplicity is at the core of the experiences they deliver."

We do not view the digital revolution as a fad or a phenomenon that will fade away rapidly. It is here to stay and will continue to define consumers and corporations over the decades to come. It is changing rapidly given the pace of technological evolution and the ability of smart, creative people to meld together diverse technologies to create very consumer compelling propositions in multiple ways.

In exploiting these new business models and the new consumer/commercial environment, we observe two types of digital player – the pure play competitors and the hybrids.

• The **pure play** competitors are generally set up by entrepreneurs who collect around them a young, agile, and creative team to reinvent the world.

  As insurgents, pure plays have little to lose and have an entirely different risk profile versus traditional players. Typically, they implement radical and ambitious strategies which incumbents find difficult to replicate given their fear of cannibalization, not to mention the inability to resolve organizational conflicts such as the meshing of Internet and traditional technology, marketing, and sales processes. The subversive economics that are available to the insurgents are often irresistible, and can wreak havoc in many industries (e.g. music distribution, newspapers, etc.) irrespective of whether or not they have long-term sustainable business models. Meanwhile some pure plays have robust and enduring business models. Think Google, AliBaba, and Amazon.

• **Hybrid** competitors already have a substantial business built on traditional business models, often involving large quantities of physical assets. These competitors have the challenge of replicating the online offers of pure plays while managing "the day job" of keeping their existing assets profitably deployed. Think Walmart, Barclays Bank, and Unilever.

As these two types of competitor battle it out, they are doing so against the backdrop of an industry landscape which is changing rapidly:

• The **changing nature of shareholder value creation** – There has been a fundamental shift in the perceptions of how shareholder value is created, at least in the early stages of the life of a pure play. The stock market has moved away from "discounted cash flow" to a "valuation based on future growth potential." Sadly for the hybrids, such valuations reward growth rather than profitability, at least in the short/medium term. Many hybrids are acutely aware of the fact that their digital businesses are not given a value anywhere close to that which a pure play, often with smaller, loss-making revenues, can command. Figure 1.3 shows the extent to which Digital/Technology businesses have dominated the value-creation agenda in the S&P 500 index, outpacing valuation growth over a ten-year period by nearly four times relative to Non Digital/Technology businesses.

• Speed as a basis of competition – Access to real-time customer reaction means that the rhythm and pace that pure plays operate under is substantially faster than traditional businesses. "A pure play will update its homepage several times a day whereas a hybrid will probably do it only once a week," said the CEO of a major British retailer.

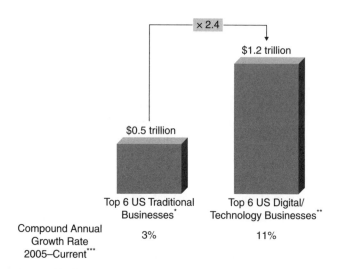

FIGURE 1.3 / Stock market valuation increases (2005 versus 2014)
Note: *Excluding banking and finance stocks and companies where data incomplete (companies included: Exxon, Walmart, General Electric, Chevron, Johnson & Johnson, and Procter & Gamble).
**Companies included: Apple, Google, Microsoft, IBM, Oracle, and Amazon.
***As of end October 2014.

We are no longer in a world where businesses can be managed by the weekly trading meeting. These have been superseded by daily trading meetings, with capability to support hourly and even real-time decision-making. Barney Harford, the CEO of Orbitz, a successful online travel business, agreed, "Pure plays innovate rapidly – we strive for hundreds of experiments on the go at any given time."

As a consequence, pure plays require organizations to be flatter and to foster speedier and less centralized decision-making. They work on the basis that daily optimization is key to winning, rather than moving forward in a more structured, timely fashion. Hybrids therefore need to worry about that old adage "the Devil takes the hindmost." It is certainly true in the digital world. Cassius Schymura of Santander's Brazilian operation observed that "Some time ago there was a tipping point in terms of companies taking online seriously – if you haven't moved yet you may have lost the race."

• Technology as a critical competence – Technology has often occupied a supporting, often back-office role in consumer-facing businesses. This is no longer the case. The organization's ability to compete on technological capability almost always distinguishes the digital winners from the also-rans. Many CEOs we interviewed acknowledge that their Chief Technology Officer (CTO) or Digital Architect was the single biggest contributor to their success. Not only that, but everyone in the organization, whether in marketing or the supply chain, now needs to be technology savvy – so technology is no longer the preserve of a single department.

Businesses need to employ people who are capable of dealing with technologies which are emerging at light-speed. The ability to meld together diverse technologies into something which the consumer can find enjoyable and simple to use has become a source of competitive advantage. Typically, technology of this nature is the domain of the young, creative, and agile mind rather than the dyed-in-the-wool, experienced IT executive. This has massive technological, organizational, and cultural implications which we will investigate later.

We will argue in subsequent chapters that the "war for talent" is a war you just have to win if you're going to succeed in the digital world. As Marc van Gelder, former CEO of Peapod, as well as Mediq in the Netherlands, observed, "Current management teams are often far too old to understand the dynamics of the digital world and the very young generation lacks managerial experience to make things happen efficiently and effectively."

A conundrum which has to be solved if you're going to win in the digital world!

• Network effects and the rise of "contested monopolies" – A new dichotomy is starting to appear in industry structures. On the one hand, it has never been easier for new competitors to enter markets rapidly, as the entry costs in the early years in many industries are relatively low. As the markets develop, rapid growth and pre-emptive market share gain is of substantial value due to the network effects and scalability that can be created. For the successful entrant, the resulting high market share and brand leader status then represents a substantial barrier to further new entrants.

What this means is that the big can get even bigger in the digital world. Equally, they need always to maintain a healthy dose of paranoia about the next new competitor who might be working away in a small garage to dethrone them. This is why we refer to them as "contested monopolies." They enjoy extremely high relative market share, and yet need to remain constantly vigilant if they are to maintain their leadership over the decades to come.

• Accelerated ability to internationalize – The rate of internationalization of many pure play businesses is breathtaking, particularly if compared to the time it took many conventional businesses such as Walmart or Visa to go global, as Figure 1.4 evidences.

These changes in landscape are changing the nature of competition and indeed strategy in many industry sectors. The idea of creating a long-term strategy and leaving it largely untouched for a few years is unlikely to

strategy and tactics begin to merge, with profound implications

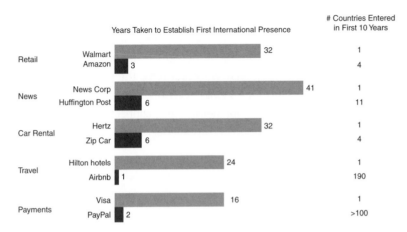

FIGURE 1.4 Pure plays have an accelerated international trajectory

be "fit for purpose" in many fast-moving, digitally-enabled sectors. In these sectors, strategy and tactics begin to merge, with profound implications. "The access to real-time data increasingly blurs the boundaries between strategy, planning and tactics – they all merge into one. In the past, you had to think about four distinct things: vision, strategy, planning and tactics. Today you only need to think about two: the vision, which is still critical, and the merging of strategy and tactics due to time compression and real-time feedback," observed Krishan Ganesh, the CEO of Big Basket in India.

It is this particular shift in the processes by which organizations have to make rapid decisions that gave us the inspiration for the title of our book – *Stractics*.

As we develop the case for a new way to manage strategy and execution in the later chapters of this book, we aim to bring these implications to life. Strategy in the digital world needs to evolve in real-time and to move quickly. Digital products can be launched and scaled in a fraction of the time that a new flavor of soup can be launched on the market.

"A digital approach allows you to test and launch products within a matter of weeks for a fraction of the investment – when strategy is being informed so quickly, it starts to look like tactics," said Prashant Tandon of HealthKart, India's premium e-health store.

We find it difficult to imagine that any company where digital/online interaction with customers is (or is likely to be) important should now be complacent about its strategy in the light of these fundamental and inexorable shifts. Indeed, Jorgen Vig Knudstorp, the CEO of Lego, reinforced this when he said, "One should never underestimate the disruptive nature of Web 3.0 where comprehensiveness, connectivity, and mobility combined to create a revolution in consumer behavior."

These shifts were admirably summarized by Tom Seery, Founder and CEO of RealSelf:

- The power of individual devices has gone up exponentially
- The world has become mobile
- Technology has changed consumer behaviors
- Consumer opinions shape the (digital) world
- We are living in a sharing economy
- Talent is increasingly scarce

In summary, entrepreneurs and investors have a huge number of opportunities, while traditional/conventional companies can enhance what they're doing by adopting radical digital strategies to either complement or replace their existing business models. Complacency is not a winning strategy, as Michael Polk, CEO at the US's Newell Rubbermaid, affirmed when he remarked that you have to believe in the digital era, and that companies who do not embrace the digital world are taking more risks versus incurring the cost of beginning to experiment and making a few mistakes.

Strategy therefore will never quite be the same again … and Stractics are here to stay.

2

Everything Needs to Change – Or Does It?

Complacency in the face of the changes that we have described could be life-threatening.

However, not everything has changed.

There are some fundamental characteristics of a successful business which are worth reflecting upon before we talk about the two types of digital combatants in the subsequent chapters. They are:

- There is a vision of where you want the business to end up – your endgame.
- The business's source of competitive differentiation/advantages is known and nurtured in order to create barriers (preferably high) to entry for others.
- The business has a high relative market share, which leads to superior profitability.
- The company has good access to capabilities and resources.
- There is a good understanding of barriers to entry and exit and how much protection they might give the business.
- The leadership has a keen sense of how the business is going to make money and create value.

All of these are "fundamental laws of gravity" and continue to underpin the development of good strategy, whether it is done for a conventional business or the more accelerated "New World" businesses.

Although these questions were almost universally ignored in the Internet bubble of the 1999–2001 era, there is a much greater preoccupation with answering them today. In the Internet bubble, the amount of money paid for businesses that had no clue about their monetization model was mind-boggling – particularly as most of it was then lost almost as quickly as it was "invested".

Only a few good companies were left standing – e.g. Google, Amazon. In those days you would not even have put Apple on that august list given that their assault on the music industry – not to mention mobile phones – had not even been designed then.

Nowadays, examples of how money can be made abound. Indeed there are many different revenue generating opportunities e.g. gross margin on sales, agency commissions/click-throughs, advertising, and service fees to name a few.

All of them have limited applicability, however, unless you are capable of capturing and retaining customers/consumers. No wonder there is a pre-occupation with customer-access models, data-mining and sophisticated loyalty schemes (to ensure consumer stickiness).

Let's consider each of these "laws" in turn:

Endgames

All strategies need to decide an ultimate endgame for the company in terms of market develop-ment, market position, product/service portfolio, geographical spread, etc. These endgames are critical to motivate the team and inspire shareholders and funders.

All strategies need to decide an ultimate endgame for the company

As we know, pure plays revel in describing heroic inroads into either exist-ing or about-to-exist markets. While they tend to be very good at creating a fuzzy photograph of this ambition, it is usually a very low resolution photograph at best. Nevertheless, it can be amazingly inspiring for those who choose to go along on the journey.

Hybrids, on the other hand, are inherently more cautious in their depiction of the future. Such caution, unfortunately, means that often they tie one of their own hands behind their backs before they even start the journey. This lack of apparent ambition has severe unintended consequences in terms of the resources that can be applied to future strategy e.g. investments, technology, and people, to name but a few. By "undercooking" the future, the competitive writing for many hybrids is often already on the wall.

Endgames are all very well but you have to be prepared to start the journey, otherwise you will never get there!

Competitive Advantage/Differentiation

Whether you are in the conventional or the digital world, you cannot get off the hook of needing to have a long-term competitive advantage or, at a minimum, some form of differentiation versus the competition. Without either of these attributes, you are a "vanilla" competitor and regrettably will suffer accordingly. Conventional strategy recognizes a number of advantages/points of differentiation that a company can adopt, e.g.:

- a superior cost position
- distinct features/capabilities of a product
- pre-emptive market share in high cost-to-enter markets
- patent/IP protection

In the digital world we can add a few:

- speed to market
- mastery of technology

- the rate of innovation and ability to adopt new technologies
- enhanced productivity resulting from a new breed of highly flexible people and/or an agile/learning culture

Traditionally, conventional businesses have not exactly been exemplary in identifying and sustaining their sources of competitive advantage/ differentiation. If anything, however, pure plays can be even worse in the sense that there is often little formal focus on these issues and how they will be developed in the future. Pure plays tend to be much more output-focused, for instance, on how many millions of customers have they touched, and how they are growing exponentially. While these are very inspiring statistics, they tell you little about the true value of the underlying business model or the financial opportunity that they might represent.

As if to prove the point, Vitor Falleiros, the Head of Planning at Dafiti, Brazil's leading online fashion company, observed, "In the online world, conviction and confidence can be competitive advantages in their own right!"

Both hybrids and pure plays would be well advised to put time aside to identify and clarify their "rationale for existing" and how their differentiation/ competitive advantage will sustain it.

Relative Market Share

In most, if not all, markets there is a clear and direct relationship between relative market share and success – usually defined as profitability! Relative market share (RMS) is calculated as your own sales divided by those of the next largest competitor or, if you are not the market leader, the sales of the market leader. Undisputed market leadership usually pertains to competitors who have a RMS greater than 1.5, while you are truly in a follower position if your RMS is less than 0.5. The logic as to why this is such an important indicator is compelling.

there is a clear and direct relationship between relative market share and success

If you are substantially larger than the next competitor, you benefit from all sorts of scale advantages with, not least, your customers. You can supplement such advantages with buying scale, manufacturing and process scale, the ability to recruit the best people, etc. In addition, there are ways of getting round the diseconomies of being subscale. Luis Maroto, CEO of Amadeus, one of the world's leading IT suppliers to the airline industry, remarked that,

> many of our clients do not have the size or resources to innovate in the digital world. Nevertheless, they need to keep up to date. Providers like Amadeus can supply the scaled technology platforms which clients can then customize to provide state-of-the-art industry solutions. We partner with them to look through the client to their consumer.

This measure, however, is not without its trials and tribulations. The most fundamental issue relates to the definition of the market. People frequently believe that this is a marketing concept, whereas in reality it has to be an economic definition driven by economic barriers to entry. If the market in which you are competing has high barriers to entry, then calculating your relative market share is applicable. If barriers to entry are low or non-existent then your definition of the marketplace is probably impractical and misleading given that scale will be defined by a broader definition of market than the one you are using.

World-Class Capabilities and Resources

Irrespective of the above, you can only compete if you have the right skills and people. This is a topic which will recur throughout this book. No strategy, either in the conventional world or in the digital world, however superior, will succeed if you try and implement it with mediocre or poorly skilled people. An essential part of strategy nowadays is The People Strategy, i.e. defining the skills that you need in order to succeed

An essential part of strategy nowadays is The People Strategy

in your particular business. If you do not get this right then any degree of theoretical competitive advantage/differentiation will remain elusive and possibly even irrelevant. Again, this is a point highlighted by Luis Maroto, CEO of Amadeus, who noted that not only his IT people had to be special. Others in the company had to upskill too: "In this new world, our sales organization has to be more sophisticated, have more proactive ideas, deal with more layers of management/joint working and strive to work with our clients to understand their consumers on a global basis."

Barriers to Entry

Especially in today's technology-disrupted world, players in any industry in any market need to be constantly aware of the permanently evolving barriers to entry for potential competitors. Market participants need to be keeping abreast of technological and other developments in order to understand what the barriers of entry are at any given moment, and what protection, or lack of it, they afford the business.

Making Money

Many pure plays put growth ahead of short term profitability … and mostly for good reason – "Often our investment decisions are driven by a view of the growth that we can add. Rapid growth matters because it is difficult to come from behind and build a market leadership position," said Nevzat Aydın, CEO of Yemeksepeti, Turkey's leading online grocery portal.

However, in the long term, monetizing the idea is a necessary evil. Evil, that is, for the entrepreneur, not for the investor, who ultimately needs to see a return on their investment. Sebastian James, the Group CEO of UK's Dixons Carphone, the UK's leading electronics retailer, pointed out that pure plays are often open to the criticism that they focus on growth, not profit/cash flow: "Pure plays' strategies are seldom about value creation in the classic sense i.e. long-term sustainable cash flow."

As noted above, nirvana for a pure play is achieved when they can describe …

- An uplifting vision,
- How their model is unique and better than any other (sustainably),
- Their high market share not only of consumers (and their revenue) but also of scarce talent that makes their product great,
- How they translate this success into market leading returns.

There are examples of companies that have achieved or appear to have achieved these lofty goals, for example, Google, Alibaba, Facebook etc. In all cases, however, we have to accept that they are in the relatively early stages of the journey and that the game is not yet fully played out.

On the hybrid side of things, there are also some business models which appear to be dynamic and successful, e.g. Dixons Carphone, The John Lewis Partnership, Williams-Sonoma, Inditex, ProSiebenSat.1, etc. Their seemingly successful defense of their traditional businesses has to be admired.

How they have achieved this will be dealt with later in this book, but we think that we can conclude that pure plays do not necessarily have the game all to themselves.

Indeed, one of the reasons why we feel that some pure plays will not "rule the roost" is that they did not adhere to some of the fundamental laws of gravity in strategy relating to:

- defining a viable endgame
- being clear about their sources of competitive advantage and differentiation
- understanding the value of (relative) market share
- investing in world-class and differentiated capabilities/resources
- understanding the barriers to entry in their market
- being able to translate their business model into a commercially viable/ attractive proposition

Without being clear about these six immutable laws of gravity, even the most cool, digital pure play might very well go up in smoke, much as many of them did at the end of the early-"noughties" dot-com boom.

In terms of investors, nothing has changed – caveat emptor is alive and well in the digital world!

3

New Business Models for the New World: Stractics in Practice

There is little debate that the digital era has created, and will continue to create, many models which will open up entirely new ways to access markets, and interact with consumers.

Before codifying and elaborating these models, it is instructive to understand why the digital era has been able to have such a fundamental impact on so many business models in so many ways.

In our opinion, this is driven by the fact that digital propositions are able to rely on four fundamental factors. These factors may be melded in different proportions in different product/propositions, but all of them are underpinning the business models of the New World in one way or another.

What are these factors?

1. **Making the complex easy to use**. Most Internet propositions are easy-to-use and intuitive. The best of them mirror consumer behavior very accurately and address fundamental consumer needs/desires. But behind these easy-to-use interfaces, the complexity of many digital propositions is considerable and includes complex technology, as well as fulfilment, customer tracking, billing systems etc. New

digital propositions essentially enable rapid and efficient matching of consumer demand with supply. But, happily, the consumer does not need to engage with this complexity.

2. **Speed**. The electronic nature of digitally-enabled interactions means that most of them are instantaneous. Stock trades are done within seconds without the need to ring up a potentially annoying, sales-oriented stockbroker. Photographs can be sent to your near ones and dear ones, without having to go down to the local shop, order prints, write a letter, and put them all in an envelope with a stamp on and go on a trip to the post office. Substantial ranges of fashion products can be browsed within minutes and an order placed within seconds. Consumers value this attribute highly.

3. **Pervasiveness**. The electronic nature of these propositions also enables multi-dimensional comprehensiveness, which is much appreciated by consumers. They span the dimensions of location and speed, as confirmed by Roger Parry, Chairman of YouGov, the new world market research company, when he said, "Mobile puts the Internet into your pocket thus releasing all the constraints of Time and Space."

   a) **Time**. Digital propositions tend to be available 24/7. You are not constrained to shop-opening hours, customer service hours, etc. You can access these propositions at any time of the day or night unconstrained by the habits and behaviors of society, or indeed other individuals.

   b) **Space**. With a few notable exceptions like China, where some services are not available, it doesn't matter where you are as long as you have a digital or WiFi connection – the service is available. This is of huge benefit to consumers, but it is also of huge benefit to the owners of the digital propositions, as it means they can achieve massive geographical reach in very short periods of time. The constraint tends not to be the digital side of these propositions. More likely, it is the fulfilment and back-office issues which limit the rate at which they can be rolled out globally.

Nevertheless they tend to achieve internationalization rates of ten to 20 times those achieved by their real-world competitors. As Eduardo Baek, a founder of eÓtica, now Brazil's leading optical retailer despite having no shops, commented, "One of the advantages of pure plays is that they can reach out to urban and remote communities which classic retail businesses cannot – and offer them a wide range of product not hitherto available to consumers."

Whether you are on your company computer, your PC at home, your smart phone at the airport or your tablet in Starbucks, the world of digital propositions is available to you.

This multi-device environment multiplies the occasions on which consumers are able to access compelling digital propositions. Little wonder that the speed at which new device propositions are taken up is now at a level which could not have been contemplated a decade ago. Imagine the supply chain complexity that Apple faces when it launches a new iPhone or iPad. Within a relatively short period of time tens of millions of these products need to reach consumers in hundreds of countries worldwide.

4. **New world economics**. The shift to digital changes the nature of the cost of doing business in a number of different ways.

Many start-ups in the digital space have very high technology cost, as they write brand new code, connecting multiple brand new technologies. In addition most of these new propositions tend to rely on access to large databases and often have to interconnect with legacy systems related to warehouse/logistics management, account management, invoicing systems, and so on. However, once you have got over the initial investment, the costs of the marginal purely digital interaction/transaction approximates to zero. For example, the cost for an online news organization to download the news to the next subscriber is close to zero.

This is not, of course, true for the hybrid or for pure plays, with substantial back offices which fulfil customers' needs, like online retailers with warehouses. It is critical when assessing the likelihood of success of pure plays (and hybrids) to understand the precise workings of the cost structure before generalizing.

When faced with fundamental shifts such as ease-of-use, cost, speed, comprehensiveness, and accessibility, it is not surprising that consumer uptake

of digital propositions is high. However, digital propositions need
to be developed and commercialized. There are a number of
new models, each of which relies on different mixes of the
above four fundamental factors. While there are many
different types of models which can be designed and
rolled out based on these four factors, we are able to
distill them into four types of business model shift. We
discuss each of these below:

Complementary/Enhancement Models

In many traditional or conventional businesses, the ability to interact with
consumers in the digital media can significantly add to the legacy proposition. The digital engagement with the customer can either deepen
their understanding of the proposition and so enhance engagement, or
alternatively add a new way of interacting to mutual advantage, thus
increasing sales. Two examples of this are given below.

1. **Consumer engagement**. Many branded consumer goods companies
   have begun to wrestle to the ground the problem of how to use digital
   means to enhance their engagement with customers (retailers) and
   consumers (users). They have harnessed the ability to enhance the
   consumers' brand perception through online digital experiences and
   to create "communities," not to mention increasing the excitement
   factors that consumers can experience through media like YouTube,
   which can be an amazingly powerful way of engaging with consumers. These fundamental shifts are well recognized by Anna Manz,
   head of strategy at one of the world's leading fast moving consumer
   goods companies, Diageo, maker of such iconic brands as Smirnoff and
   Johnnie Walker. "Our customers are now living their lives differently
   and faster – as a consequence we have to be more entrepreneurial,
   innovate faster, and seek to have impact faster." It is clearly possible to
   communicate much more about the brand and its meaning if you can
   persuade the consumer to spend five minutes on your website rather
   than the normal few seconds that a broadcast advert spot would give

you. In addition, the amount of information and "colour" that you can communicate about your product and brand is massively enhanced. Finally, the ability to process huge amounts of transaction data to better understand your consumer is an opportunity that few fast-moving consumer goods (FMCG) companies should forego.

As Desirée Bollier, CEO of Value Retail PLC Group explained,

> We are one of very few businesses who have consciously decided not to pursue e-commerce because we believe our strategic advantage comes from making our outlet villages truly magical for customers. Despite this, digital is an integral element of our strategy and one in which we invest substantially – we have a Digital team of 60, focused purely on customer engagement through content, editorial and digital channels; our marketing budget has gone from 5% to 50% digital

2. **Multichannel shopping**. Many retail companies now regard online shopping as "business as usual." The ability to allow consumers to purchase products at any time of the day or night from any of their devices significantly enhances the reach of that retailer. In addition, it is possible to display many more stock keeping units (SKUs) online than you could reasonably stock in any one store, and you can communicate very much more product information, including provenance, sizes, etc., than would be possible on a label on a product. Similarly it is possible to promote products in an entirely different way online. Combine this with a home delivery service and you have a great formula for enhancing customer experience and satisfaction.

In some sectors of the retail industry there is a very healthy interplay between the physical world and the digital world. The former provides a consumer with the possibility of seeing, touching, and experiencing the product; while in the latter case their final decision can be communicated online quickly and conveniently to the vendor. Everybody wins. John Lewis and Argos are two notable examples in the UK who do this expertly, despite having very different philosophies/roles for the physical channel.

In both of these examples, the digital/online experience is enhancing the traditional business model, as opposed to trying to replace it. The consumer is substantially better off, even though their fundamental perceptions of what is provided by the FMCG company or the retailer have not necessarily been radically changed.

Extension of the Existing Business Model

By taking advantage of the data availability and lower-cost, electronic distribution capability of digital propositions, the existing core business model of a traditional/conventional company can be rapidly and substantially enhanced.

the existing core business model of a traditional/ conventional company can be rapidly and substantially enhanced

We offer two examples of this extension:

1. **Extending market reach through the re-segmentation of the market**. The low cost and the ubiquity of digital/online propositions allow the identification of, access to, and serving of new segments of the market which were hitherto beyond the reach of the conventional/ traditional business model. For instance, Net-A-Porter, the online fashion retailer, has added Outnet and Mr Porter to cater for different customer segments and missions.
2. **Geographic expansion**. Digital propositions are relatively easy to deploy in geographic regions where physical access might be expensive or otherwise difficult to achieve. Hybrids can often achieve rapid expansion within a country by offering their products online. Department store players such as Neiman Marcus now enjoy considerable online sales (more than 40% of their total) originating from regions where they don't have stores.

Internationally, the same holds true. Traditionally, a retailer who wished to expand abroad faced a complex, expensive, and time-consuming process requiring a lot of planning, research on the ground, identification and negotiation of suitable sites, store fit-out, recruitment of sales staff, replenishment of the store, etc. This was typically a process with high capital and operating costs.

Compare this process with a digital online experience being extended geographically between the home country and a new market where often the only adjustments that need to be made pertain to language, currency, and the identification of a suitable fulfilment operation. It is therefore not surprising that the rate of internationalization of online retail businesses is an order of magnitude higher than that experienced by traditional physical store retailers. Businesses such as Asos, for instance, have achieved substantial revenues from international markets in a fraction of the time taken by store-based retailers.

Market Disruption

Sometimes the four distinguishing factors of the digital/online world combine to create very compelling models which can substitute in part or whole for traditional/conventional business models. Barney Harford, the CEO of Orbitz, confirmed this: "Pure plays can pursue disruptive strategies, particularly if they are well branded, focused on applications, on scaling up internationally, and dealing with loyalty issues in a way that the hybrids/traditional companies cannot."

We earlier mentioned the fact that basic retail banking is moving rapidly from a branch-based business to an online business. Consumers can get access to their bank accounts, transfer money, receive money, and move money between current and savings products in one "touch." The convenience involved in this is substantial and hence it is little wonder that most UK and American banks are progressively closing their branch networks or alternatively transforming them in such a way that they move away from basic banking products to complex products or enhanced cross-selling opportunities. This process will accelerate, with the result that many aspects of conventional retail banking will only be available online. Cheques have already been discontinued by many banks, and the issuing of paper bank statements is probably pretty close behind.

There are many examples of big market disruption, including the identification of and access to lawyers in the United States. Indeed it is also happening with doctors in Europe, as noted by Artur Smolarek, Managing Director, Health Insurance Division at PZU Poland, who said, "Feedback from customers is becoming more and more important. The quality and rating of doctors can now become an important differentiating factor in terms of customer oriented value propositions."

And it can happen in seemingly simple businesses like taxis as well!

Uber's very simple taxi-ordering smartphone application is in the process of disrupting many traditional taxi businesses around the world. Indeed in Germany the impact has been so profound that there has been a significant backlash from the taxi industry, which is attempting to get the service banned on the basis of passenger safety.

New, New

Given the power of the transformation that digital enables, it would be very surprising if new marketplaces were not identified and developed.

it would be very surprising if new marketplaces were not identified and developed

The emergence of entirely new ways of communicating, sharing, and interacting, such as Facebook, Twitter, and WhatsApp, attests to the vibrancy and creativity of the digital world. These propositions have created huge marketplaces for communication. On the back of these marketplaces there will, no doubt, be opportunities for massive monetization. The fact that each of these new businesses interact with hundreds of millions of people offers huge and hitherto unknown opportunities for engaging with consumers. The precise way in which this will happen is still emerging, but given the creativity and drive of those individuals looking at these opportunities, we have no doubt that business models will emerge which will allow for their monetization.

When one looks back over the last five years, one sees an inexorable march of new ideas, new business models, and new ways of accessing and engaging with consumers.

To conclude this chapter we wanted to share with you in Table 3.1 some of the most notable examples of innovative pure plays of recent years. They are primarily "Disruptive" or "New, New" propositions.

These innovative models are compelling and disruptive. One would conclude that hybrids have much to fear. However, all is not lost, as hybrids can emulate some aspects of the new digital models, as we will argue in later chapters. In the meantime, suffice it to say that we agree with Richard Pennycook, the CEO of the Co-op group in the UK, when he said, "There is nothing new in disruption – it is a natural law of gravity in business. The interesting thing is what sort of disruption it is – the digital revolution is a capital-light disruption and therefore can occur very rapidly at very low cost."

TABLE 3.1   **Example of notable innovative digital businesses in the last 10 years**

2004–2008		2009–2013	
Company	**Company Description**	**Company**	**Company Description**
Kayak	Comparative travel search engine	Square	Online financial services provider
BlaBlaCar	Europe car-sharing platform	Quirky	Invention-sharing platform
Yelp	Crowd-sourced review platform for local businesses	Kickstarter	Global crowd-funding platform focused on creative projects
Wonga	Online British payday loan company	Uber	Private ridesharing website connecting passengers with drivers of vehicles
ZocDoc	US online medical care scheduling service	WhatsApp	Global instant messaging application service for mobiles
Zyngo	Social gaming services provider	Nest	Home thermostat online automation company
Living-social	Online marketplace to buy and share information on local activities	Flipboard	Social-network aggregation, magazine format mobile application
Groupon	Local deal-of-the-day website	Citymapper	Improved transport application
Airbnb	Global network for renting accommodation offered by locals	Coursera	Educational technology company offering online courses
Dropbox	File-hosting services company	Oyster	Streaming service company for books

4
chapter

Pure Plays and How
They Change the World

In terms of industry development and competitive transformation, the Internet era has been an unprecedented period. The pace at which consumers have changed attitudes, new business models have been developed/introduced, and new competitors have risen (and in some cases fallen) is breathtaking.

To some extent we were given some insight into how this might develop during the 1999–2001 dot-com era.

Despite these early indicators of what might lie ahead digitally, we think that most of our interviewees have been overwhelmed either positively or negatively by the scale and pace of online development over the last decade. Massive companies have been created (Facebook) while others have been brought to their knees (some booksellers – think Borders; some directories – think *Yellow Pages*).

This massive transformation of the competitive landscape has mostly been inspired by pure plays, i.e. companies who only have online activities and who are therefore not encumbered by either the assets or the organizational inertia of most incumbent/traditional companies.

For most pure plays, barriers to entry were quite low – at least in the early stages of the development of their markets. Stores did not have to be found/bought, factories did not have to be built, and sales forces did not have to be recruited and trained. All in all, the cost of entry was modest. In addition, the target customer base was usually well defined and could be targeted easily. Marketing and customer access costs could be significant, but seldom penal.

Purely digital entry which is focused on delivering what the customer really, really wants can succeed. We agree with Spencer Rascoff, CEO of Zillow, the leading online real estate information provider in the US marketplace, when he said, "competitive advantage resides in your ability to exploit technology (e.g. being early into mobile) and any scale advantages, particularly in advertising and public relations. More importantly you have to exploit your cumulative experience in bringing the right products to your consumer base."

Most of these pure play businesses focus on growth rather than profit or earnings before interest, taxes, depreciation and amortization (EBITDA). Inherently their objective is to create a leading and often unassailable market-share position, and their investors are happy to support them. Only later in the life-cycle of the company would they turn to the thorny issue of how to monetize these market positions.

And they invest accordingly, as Spencer Rascoff of Zillow confirmed: "For pure plays, valuation often drives investment criteria. Revenue growth is critical and hence we are able to allocate, say, $5 million for something which is relatively experimental. Taking such a substantial and financial risk would be difficult for a hybrid to contemplate given their relatively tight financial controls."

These criteria were confirmed by Alexander Kudlich, Board Member, Group Managing Director, of the Internet investment company Rocket Internet: "Perquisites for every investment decision are attractive unit economics and significant market potential. We identify a proven business model, roll out the companies to different markets around the world, and scale them into market leadership positions. Our metrics are month-on-month growth, growth of market share, and improving unit economics. Growing market share is particularly important for those digital businesses that operate in the 'winner takes all' markets."

Having achieved such a high relative market share, it is almost inevitable that the cost of entry for the second and third waves of entrants – whether they are pure plays or hybrids – can be prohibitive.

By their very nature, pure plays are usually populated by younger, more risk-taking individuals who have a passion for what they are doing and a more intuitive understanding of the needs of their potential customer base. These teams are more agile and creative then their traditional counterparts. They are also driven less by economic gain than by fame/notoriety.

More importantly these companies are led by visionaries who have a mission to change the world. They are bold, as was evidenced by a conversation with Google's Northern and Central European VP, Matt Brittin, who said, "We are interested in opportunities that can change our business by ten times, not 10%." These leaders raise the competitive bar substantially and create new benchmarks which many traditional companies find difficult to comprehend and respond to. Robert Hohman, CEO of glassdoor, also had suitably bold objectives, "We want to be the world's largest career community – a share of market vision. Anywhere I've ever worked, the vision had to be a BHAG (Big Hairy Audacious Goal). Something really inspiring, almost unattainable."

The inherently responsive and flexible business models that these new leaders create invariably focus on a bold vision of the future. Few of them, however, would have a strategy or a three-year business plan that would be recognized by conventional management teams. Having set out the vision, much else of what they do tends to be experimental and empirical. They are constantly challenging their own understanding about what customers want and how they behave, often reinventing themselves almost as quickly as they came into being in the first place. They tend to be obsessed by what their customers want.

The nature of the online world allows them to design new products rapidly and frequently, given the possibility of testing them online almost in real time with subgroups of customers. Customer feedback is rapid and insightful in terms of the acceptability/attractiveness of the

Customer feedback is rapid and insightful

proposition. Such feedback has become critical in the development and refinement of new propositions. Indeed, customers are part of the co-creation process pursued by many pure plays.

This preoccupation ultimately translates into an appropriate obsession with consumers/customers, with which Rogério Takayanagi, the CEO of TIM Fiber in Brazil, agreed: "Pure plays add value through customer knowledge and processing insight rapidly through customer relationship management (CRM). At the end of the day, it's normally consumers who drive change." By definition, pure plays have a greater focus on the future than on the present. And they are in a hurry.

They value speed rather than perfection and are constantly open to the concept of reinventing themselves if that's what consumers and customers require. Some of our interviewees indicated that the pure play phenomenon has given rise to two new sources of competitive advantage, namely speed and culture.

In terms of describing the digital landscape, we would go further.

Our interviews and analysis indicate that pure plays often represent a new type of competitor. One which encompasses a new series of approaches and paradigms, encompassing the following qualities:

1. **Bold creative visions**. Pure plays truly think about reinventing the world, or at least that bit of the world in which they are competing. Those who head up and found these businesses tend to be young iconoclasts who wish to leave their marks on the industries in which they compete. They rethink old paradigms, imagine the impossible, and generally turn historical ways of doing business on their heads. Not only do they rethink consumer propositions and the resulting business models, they also knit together technologies in a way not hitherto contemplated. The results of these approaches can often be both breathtakingly simple but also breathtakingly different. As Barney Harford, the CEO of Orbitz, noted, "Pure plays, despite being smaller, can be much more innovative and disruptive."

2. **Pace and the sense of urgency**. The leaders of these new businesses and paradigms tend to be in a hurry. Once they have the breakthrough

idea they want to implement it rapidly, and not only in their domestic market but in as many markets as will take it. The rate at which these new models are rolled out, both domestically, and often internationally, leave the hybrids well behind. "Be quick and iterate – opportunities abound but not forever," observed Yu Gang, the co-founder and Chairman of Yihaodian, one of China's leading e-commerce players.

This sense of pace and urgency is not merely a reflection of the impatience of the founder but possibly also the result of very astute commercial thinking – if models can be rolled out quickly, why wouldn't you do it? The value of high and pre-emptive market share has been demonstrated time and time again in the conventional commercial markets. Why wouldn't it also work in the new digital world?

Pace also provides a competitive advantage for pure plays, as noted by Robert Hohman, CEO of glassdoor, a high-growth Silicon Valley business, "One of the advantages that pure plays have is that hybrids tend to move slowly and late."

3. **Focus and Flexibility**. The entrepreneurs who create pure plays are certainly very single-minded about their visions, but are also entirely pragmatic about how to deliver them. The many ways in which technologies can be knitted together, and the speed at which technologies change means that successful digital propositions are tested and iterated rapidly in order to refine their product and business model. Failure in the cause of perfecting the business model is acceptable as long as it takes the game forward; tactical moves therefore intimately impact strategy and its delivery.

Stractics has become a reality.

Stractics has become a reality.

4. **Technology**. As we will mention a number of times later on in this book, technology is not to be confused with conventional IT. The sort of technologies which are being developed in the digital world (search, file sharing, instant messaging, behavior tracking, etc.) have little to do with traditional IT systems, which tend to be very back-office-oriented. Technology in the digital world is much more to do with consumer functionality and interface. The secret is often knitting technologies together, rather than inventing a brandnew technology. Technologies

also seem to come and go rapidly, hence the classic two-to-three-year IT systems project has very little to do with rapid-fire empirical development and implementation of new customer-oriented ideas. Little wonder, therefore, that new skills, organizations, and cultures need to be developed to handle this new approach.

Indeed, many pure plays regard themselves as consumer-oriented technology companies. They therefore employ a disproportionate number of technologically adept people, whether they are engineers, developers, or software experts. They spend money entirely in sync with the belief that they are technology companies. Amazon for instance spends approximately 7–8% of sales on technology, versus many hybrid retailers who would feel uncomfortable spending more than 2% of sales.

This preoccupation with technology makes them into formidable competitors who can move at speed. Nevertheless, as Roy Amara, a researcher and scientist at Stanford Research Institute and the Institute for the Future, said, "We tend to overestimate the impact of a technology in the short run and underestimate the effect in the long run."

Technology can however be a double-edged sword. As pure plays grow, it can also be a challenge. Peter Plumb, CEO of the UK's moneysupermarket.com, recognized that "in terms of scaling up, technology becomes the major obstacle. Acquiring technology talent and upgrading systems which were originally designed for a small business can be massive obstacles."

- **Culture**. the people who are good at doing all of these things tend to be slightly less conventional, a lot younger and considerably more flexible than the average employee of most traditional/conventional businesses. Their objectives are often much more complicated than merely being interested in short-term financial rewards and their long-term career.

The digital wave is populated by such people "who want to make a difference," and hence need to be managed in ways which are entirely alien to many classical HR policies. They do not necessarily want to be constrained to the standard nine-to-five working day, they need space to think/create/play, they need an environment which is tolerant of experimentation (and sometimes failure), and they need to be motivated by their own and their team's success, not just by the success of the business.

And you sometimes have to adopt new rules. Jonathan Gabbai, Head of International Mobile Product at eBay, recommended, "Tolerating a reasonably high failure rate is good and being rewarded for trying things out is absolutely necessary."

Businesses which do not respond to this and do not therefore spend time creating the right culture will not only fail to attract the right talent, they will just plain old fail. Rick Hamada, CEO of Avnet in the US, put it very succinctly when he said, "in the digital age, culture eats strategy for lunch every day of the week."

We would also note that the talent pool within pure play organizations often tends to be far more skilled. Figure 4.1 is fairly stark in depicting both the pay and productivity differentials across digital and non-digital businesses. If you have populated your organization with the brightest talent, which is well remunerated, your likelihood of succeeding is

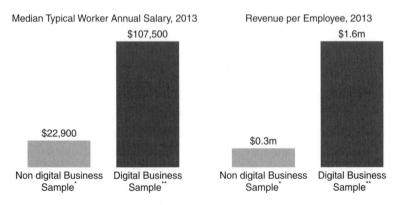

FIGURE 4.1 / **Salary and revenue per employee**

Note: *Walmart and Walgreens's average
**Apple and Google's average

heightened. This also enables pure plays to adopt flatter structures with more decentralized decision-making.

And this difference in salary is well worth it, as confirmed by James Meekings, Founder of Funding Circle: "Talent is an issue – the gap between mediocre versus great people is huge, and getting great people, particularly technology people, is the key." A senior pure play executive agreed when he confirmed that he is in a people/talent war, often spending up to two days of his week interviewing people and trying to find those who think differently and move faster.

Little wonder that hybrids should be fearful of their pure play counterparts. They have changed the nature of Strategy to a world of Stractics: implementing and "fast cycling" tactical moves to inform and create their strategies.

But, as we shall see later, pure plays do have their own challenges. Many of these relate to how they move from being a small start-up to being a fully-fledged member of one of the world's stock markets. As Stefan Winners, board member of Germany's Burda Digital Holding, observed, "The more rapid pace of the digital world requires the board and the shareholders to control more frequently and make sure that actions are taken as a consequence."

pure plays do have their own challenges

And scaling up can be expensive, thus limiting the options available to the normally cash-poor pure plays. As Mark Britton, Founder of Avvo, the innovative lawyers online business in the US, observed,

> Even though valuations are a psychological issue and people can become giddy about the future, thus creating high valuations, this can work both ways for pure plays given that they have trouble knowing the exact right way of scaling up. As they are small companies, they have to choose one path while bigger companies (hybrids) can choose three or four paths forward … And fund them. The role of the CEO is therefore critical, as he has to be vigilant about the path and transparent with his team about the uncertainties so that he instils trust from his team that he will make the right decision.

He also has to manage risk on behalf of his or her investors, as evidenced by Alexander Kudlich, Board Member, Group Managing Director, Rocket Internet, when he said: "Assuming that the opportunity is large enough, we then focus on minimizing risk – business model risk, financing risk, and execution risk. In the digital world, where everything changes with the speed of light, another crucial component to winning is speed … And of course working harder than the competition!"

And so while pure plays appear to have many advantages, as they are untrammeled by legacy issues, success comes from hard work on many fronts, as observed by Yu Gang, co-founder and Chairman of Yihaodian: "As a pure play, we have the following challenges:

- how to maintain an outstanding customer experience in the light of burgeoning competition,
- how to acquire the right talent in an overheated Chinese market,
- how to avoid the dilutions of the corporate culture as we grow,
- how to make sure that our marketplace merchants do not undermine our proposition, for example, by selling 'fakes' on our site."

Rick Hamada, CEO of Avnet, would add one challenge: "Even pure plays must have an ultimate path to financial success and therefore the identification of what performance levels will have to be met to deliver that success needs to be an early priority."

5
chapter

Hybrid Players – Waking up to the New Digital Reality!

For hybrid players – conventional companies where there is increasingly an e-commerce/digital element – there is often an instinct to do as little as possible until a digital threat is truly evident. They worry primarily about the fact that moving online might involve the reduction of their more conventional/traditional activities. All too seldom do hybrids consider digital to be a big opportunity which could open up access to new sources of growth.

A pure play executive pointed to the lack of realism sometimes demonstrated by some retailers when he observed that hybrids are often thoughtful about digital but fail to get people who understand how it will affect their business world. Indeed, he felt that many retailers look at digital as an arena where common sense and logic do not apply.

This is a very parochial perspective in terms of competition, and one that has been proven time and time again to lead to competitive disaster. For instance, it has often been demonstrated that cannibalization is best done to yourself. However painful it is, it will be a lot less painful than someone else doing it to you. "In the digital world, traditional businesses are threatened by the fact that barriers to entry drop. Nevertheless content, brand, customer relationships, etc., continue to have significant value. Hybrids have historically underestimated these assets and therefore suffer from a lack of courage in cannibalizing their own revenues and building for the future," said Derk Haank, CEO of the scientific publisher Springer.

But cannibalization remains very tough because one tends to be asking experienced (but possibly poorly informed about the digital world) senior executives to consider committing the commercial equivalent of Hara-kiri. Seldom do they think that the digital world creates exciting business models which will generate equally exciting opportunities for growth, and profit! Sir Martin Sorrell, CEO of global media company WPP, understands the need to cannibalize and develop in line with the market. "In the digital age, we all have to cannibalize ourselves in a sensible but timely way. WPP can pride itself on the fact that much of its current revenue did not exist a few years ago – to that extent we operate as a strategic venture capitalist, constantly reinventing ourselves."

"Doing nothing," however, is life-threatening!

As Jerry Buhlmann, CEO of media-buying giant Dentsu Aegis Network, observed: "The biggest risk in traditional business models is not grasping the digital opportunity."

As hybrids, with a seemingly bewildering kaleidoscope of technologies to choose from, and equally constant changes in consumer behavior to adapt to, they need to take on the digital opportunity in a logical but open-minded (and open-eyed) way. Jeff Holzschuh, vice-chairman of Morgan Stanley, was sure that this is right – "Conviction is critical – the digital revolution is here, we just have to make it part of our evolutionary imperatives."

There are, however, some logical questions which hybrids should be asking about consumers, markets, and competitors and their economics. In fact we think there are two vital questions:

• What is happening in the increasingly digital marketplace?
• What should we be doing about it?

In the first half of this chapter we will address both of these questions in a relatively clinical fashion.

In the second half we will turn to the knotty problems associated with turning relatively logical and seemingly straightforward answers into reality. In other words we will address the major challenges hybrids face as they move into the digital world.

However, let us start with the two logical questions.

What is Happening in the Increasingly Digital Market Place?

Understanding the (increasingly digital) marketplace – and most importantly, consumers within these markets – requires a new approach and potentially a new set of capabilities.

When assessing markets and opportunity, hybrids have traditionally focused on market size, channels to market, etc. In the digital world, there needs to be a much greater obsession with customer/consumer behavior, including how they will respond to online (and offline) propositions and how this behavior will change over time. This understanding is critical as it will set the agenda for the market opportunity for the hybrid, the nature of the required proposition, the need for innovation (and what type of innovation), and the urgency of response.

Above all, hybrids (and pure plays) need to follow the customer.

> "Consumers are now more important to listen to than retailers and hence the real revolution here is in consumer power. Hybrids need to understand that brands can be made or destroyed by consumers who are very articulate about what they like and do not like, and do not hesitate to feed this back to anyone who will listen," said Mothercare CEO Mark Newton-Jones,

In assessing the market, hybrids have to change the way they evaluate market opportunity and the activity within those markets. Metrics like average transaction value and purchase frequency, as a way of understanding customer performance and how to drive it, are no longer adequate. In the digital world, consumer behavior is critical and hence we need to understand it, and how to create interactions with the consumer that will persuade them that you have the "go to" site for your particular category of products/propositions. The objective is to discover how you will become a "habit" within the shoppers' lives.

So if you are operating your digital business as one that only has intermittent connection with its consumers, think hard about your business model. It won't be long before you will be made redundant by a company whose product/proposition has become a habit and part of your consumers' purchasing repertoire.

"Digital is all about the customer/consumer identifying their needs, establishing focus and creating loyalty," emphasizes Sebastian James, the Group Chief Executive of Dixons Carphone.

Jonathan Gabbai, Head of International Mobile Product at eBay, agreed:

> Having a rapid response team with the sole goal of tackling customer experience issues that emerge on a daily basis through feedback from sources such as contact centers, social media, etc., is absolutely required. This needs to be a team who can go in and fix code, streamline the user experience, and unblock the complexity in a customer issue. It needs to be cross functional.

Even traditionally B2B businesses such as Experian, the global credit services giant, are having to think about consumers as much as they did about their clients/customers. Brian Cassin, Experian's CEO, confirmed this when he said, "In the digital world you have to focus on the consumer journey and make your models much more consumer oriented. Increasingly our products focus on the consumer rather than the customer (the intermediary) and are designed to empower the consumer to get better outcomes for themselves. With this in mind, our traditional customers will also be even more enthusiastic about our product suite as it will increasingly delight their customers – the consumer."

The evaluation of market opportunities/threats has therefore changed fundamentally versus hybrids' previous styles of thinking.

What Should We be Doing about It?

In terms of thinking about what to do about it, an early priority is to translate these market-/consumer-related insights into objectives and timelines for the company, while at the same time understanding that these will change over time as experimentation occurs in the market-place, both by yourselves and your competitors. As we have already argued, the ability to experiment and to respond at pace is fundamental to success in the digital/online world.

These new organizational characteristics require the design of a winning business model which will deliver the new digital strategy. Traditionally, strategy was about the choice of product/market segment that a business chose to enter. Now it is about designing models which have the ability to move fast and economically in order to address the constantly changing set of consumer desires in a much more rapid fashion than was required in their traditional businesses. As Jerry Buhlmann, CEO of Dentsu Aegis Network said, "Digital is all about innovating your proposition – adding value by doing things differently, better and faster."

It is sobering to note, but it will not always be possible to define a winning business model. In some sectors, the competitive landscape will cause great concern, given that it will be clear that some pure play insurgents will be very low-cost commodity providers whose advance could have devastating consequences for current incumbents who will not be able to replicate the low cost pure play business model fast enough or well enough.

In other sectors it will be possible for traditional players to add value beyond that which an online player can.

For instance, in some retail sectors where complex product innovation is rife (e.g. smart TVs), physical demonstration is all-important, irrespective of whether the final purchase is made in-store or online. In these sectors, suppliers will recognize the cost incurred by the retailer to maintain physical presence and hence reward them appropriately. Nevertheless, they will also want their products to be available both offline and online – the hybrid, however, may very well be better placed to deliver this channel proposition than a pure play.

"Hybrids should not underestimate their value to suppliers, particularly in businesses where innovation is important, and being able to showcase the product enhances the consumer experience," said Sebastian James of Dixons Carphone.

It is therefore incumbent upon the hybrid player to understand the nature of the marketplace such that they can work out whether there truly is a future for hybrids in the sector or whether "the game is already up."

In particular, they need to refer to the business models we described in the earlier chapter and ask whether the model they need to adopt is the one which is complementary, enhancing or disruptive of their existing model and business. Once this thinking is done, then the redefinition of the hybrid's new business model and the way forward will be a lot clearer – but not, unfortunately, a lot easier. As Dr Hillebrand, vice-chairman of the executive board of Otto observed, "In the digital world hybrids have to start early to completely rethink their entire strategy starting from scratch. We are living in the New World – the components of a good strategy are completely different nowadays."

Challenges for the Hybrid

The complexity of the challenges facing hybrids in terms of reacting to the new world requirements – obsession with the customer, mastery of new technologies, fast decision-making, etc. – cannot be overestimated. We list here the four most critical areas in which hybrids struggle.

1. **People, structure and culture:**

We have already mentioned how "digital people" are different – and need to be managed differently – versus those in the traditional business environment. They are more creative, impatient, informal, and technologically astute, and are motivated by very different objectives than those in the traditional commercial environment. As Guilherme Loureiro, CEO of Walmart Brazil commented, "Traditional businesses need to accept that in their early stages of going online they need different people, possibly more highly rewarded and certainly growth oriented versus traditional businesses."

This talent pool is very different from the traditional talent pool in most companies, as noted by Michael Hansen, CEO of Cengage, a leading educational publisher, when he said: "One of the key differentiating factors between winners and losers in the digital world is the acquisition of technology talent. Building an internal culture that provides technology with a strong sense of impact and 'cause' is key to attracting and retaining talent beyond the current average of two years. Competitive compensation alone is not enough."

The culture in which they will operate most effectively tends to be less structured, flatter, and with rapid response mechanisms built in. For instance, decisions can be made rapidly, and quite often by people more junior, than in a conventional organizational structure. Similarly, it is necessary to recognize that the individuals who tend to be good operators in the digital world tend to be resistant to formal authority structures, and the classical application of primarily financial incentive schemes. If you do not reflect these differences in your "digital culture," you will pretty soon not have a "digital capability." It will walk out of the door, as emphasized by Mike Walsh, CEO at Lexis Nexis, when he said "talent is a huge issue – where you get it, how you compensate it and how you create a culture which will retain it not to mention creating an environment where it will be productive are critical issues."

In addition, experimentation – and from time to time, failure thereof – needs to be an integral part of the business system. Andrew Crawley, Chief Commercial Officer of British Airways, was clear on this point: "Experimentation is important and therefore you have to have permission to fail, which can only come from the top."

Leaders in hybrid companies who want digital to thrive, therefore, need to rethink the way they organize the company and de-emphasize classical functional structures. Rather they should focus more on the organizational principles that enable decisions to be made at pace, which foster innovation, and which enable swift response to competitor activity. This calls for a marked shift from individual departments that are excellent in their own right, to more cross functional team-based working that can get things done without having to move through layers of hierarchy. Digital companies typically have half as many levels before CEO when compared to the traditional norm.

For these reasons, the leadership role is critical in hybrids. Jan Bayer, Board member of Germany's Axel Springer, was very clear about his prerequisites for success:

> A successful strategy for the digital world needs to be created at the top:
>
> - The CEO has to lead by living a more digital culture – e.g. write your own emails!
> - Be consistent in your messaging.
> - Be bold – you need to take more radical actions if you want to drive growth and an improved bottom line.
> - You need complete alignment of the shareholders and the board.

And below the CEO there can be profound shifts in the way a company operates. "As traditional businesses become hybrids, they need to accept that their company will have less structure, and possibly, less discipline, and certainly fewer experienced people, and possibly more junior people. The rhythms and routines of the business will need to change," said Mark Newton-Jones, the CEO of Mothercare, a major British retailer of children's apparel and accessories.

One technique used by a number of hybrids is to establish their embryonic online activities in a separate unit. The CEO of the UK's Home Retail

Group, John Walden, explained how it works: "In the early years you may need to set up parallel organizations in order to get up and running in the online world. The online team needs to educate the rest of the company and not be smothered by them." Toon Bouten, CEO of Tomorrow Focus AG, agreed: "Hybrids have to build pure play units in parallel to their traditional businesses, ultimately integrating them, or in exceptional cases allowing the digital unit to overtake the traditional business."

However, long term, Dan Mallin at Magnet 360 had two observations:

- "Your digital strategy has to be implemented across the business not just in marketing!
- Most companies have someone thinking about digital, but few have everyone thinking about it!"

2. **Technology and innovation:**

Technology is at a premium in the digital world.

Successful digital players (hybrids or pure plays) have built substantial in-house technology capabilities, see these as a cornerstone of their success, and invest heavily. The number of technology staff as a proportion of the total headcount is often double or quintupled in digitally inclined businesses. For instance, many leading e-commerce players have more web developers than category managers/merchants.

Hybrids have a particular challenge in terms of attracting the right sort of people into their companies. In addition, they have the problem of integrating the new-wave technology approaches into often rather traditional IT structures. Such organizations are not necessarily known for their flexibility and innovative approaches. Rather they are structured around very large, multi-year systems projects which bear little resemblance to the type of fast moving technology associated with today's pure plays. Brian Cassin, CEO of credit services giant, Experian, reinforced this point when he said, "In terms of technology, you have to separate product development from back-office systems. The former has to be very agile and responsive while the latter may take longer to transform."

Often, therefore, it is not only necessary to create a parallel technology organization – at least initially, it is also necessary to introduce new rules which will encourage innovation, and fast innovation at that. Similarly, it will be necessary to tolerate experimentation, failure, and rapid redirection in these new, agile, and fast-moving units in order to make sure that technology is keeping pace and even driving consumer acceptance of the product/proposition.

3. **Investment, risk, decision-making, and pace:**

Very few digital businesses would still be around if the investment decisions to establish and grow them had been based purely on NPV, IRR, and traditional thresholds of returns normally found in more traditional hybrids.

Whilst these criteria are not obsolete, the rate of change created by the digital world requires that decision-making and investment approvals are partly based on belief and conviction in the opportunity, rather than solely on a set of financial business cases. This calls for a more flexible approach to investment decision-making and a different attitude to risk. "A lot of our financial investments are conviction-based, and we consider factors such as the cost of not automating something in helping us to develop the logical case for investment," said Tim Steiner, CEO of Ocado, the UK's online-only grocery retailer. Also, companies need to recognize different ways of doing things. Roger Parry, Chairman of YouGov, observes that

> Digital is all about remembering the fundamentals of economics and finance. Part of the problem for hybrids is that they have to expense most things through the P&L, whilst some pure play 'acqui-hires' (acquisition of companies with highly valued/skilled teams of people) allow the acquisition of talent to be financed by the balance sheet.

This was confirmed by Mike Walsh, CEO of Lexis Nexis: "For hybrids, particularly those that are highly financially managed, a key issue is how fast can you improve performance in such a way that you can fund innovation."

You can therefore forgive many hybrids for thinking that investments in the digital world are more uncertain and difficult to assess than those in their traditional businesses. This is indeed the conventional wisdom. However, most of our interviewees believe that this is a gross simplification. Roger Parry, Chairman of YouGov, is clear on this point, "It is a myth that digital businesses find it difficult to put together robust business plans." Jim Lawrence, former Chairman of Rothschild North America, and a non-executive director at IAG, owner of British Airways, agreed: "In terms of being able to build business cases in the digital world, there is no excuse for not having a good product and a convincing and well-supported argument."

For instance, whilst it may appear to be safer to invest in a physical store, for instance, the consumer data underpinning such decisions is often just as uncertain as that behind many digital investments. Indeed, it is increasingly the case that there is enough experience with digital propositions to regard the data as more and more reliable. And thanks to "big data," the ability of digital players (including hybrids) to collect and process huge amounts of information about their consumers' behaviors means that they are increasingly well placed to make well-supported business cases and decisions. Indeed, Guilherme Loureiro, the CEO of Walmart Brazil, confirmed that "online, data becomes a major differentiator. If you cannot process and gain insight from customer data, you have little competitive advantage."

Experience, too, is a factor in online investment decisions. This was underlined by Barney Harford, the CEO of Orbitz, who said, "To an offline or hybrid player, technology investments can be seen as highly risky, as they don't have the experience in making that kind of investment. They haven't made enough progress down the learning curve to be able to invest as confidently as the online pure plays, which tend to be much more comfortable making technology bets, as they have much experience making them, and they've learned how to manage projects to increase predictability and reduce risk."

But sometimes you may need to trust your judgment – Andy Street, managing director of one of the most successful omni-channel retailers in the UK, The John Lewis Partnership, said, "Traditionally, risk in our business has been location-specific, but now it is a lot less determinate. Sometimes you have to apply judgment and 'just roll the dice' rather than be left behind."

Matt Brittin, VP of Google Northern and Central Europe, agreed:

> We need to identify and bet on the long-term trends – video, mobile, social, and whatever comes next. Investment decisions need to be based on belief about where one could create competitive advantage – if you have the choice between being slow and 100% right, or fast and 80% right, take the faster option! For a pure play, the investment criteria are less rigid than for hybrids. You need to believe that the investment supports the long-term vision. Certainly you need some analysis but you need conviction even more.

And to add pressure to the situation, all of the above needs to be undertaken at a pace entirely untypical of many traditional businesses. "Traditional businesses need to move at lightspeed in order to defend against or overtake pure play insurgents," asserted Keith Allen, COO of Mecom, a Dutch/Danish newspaper group. Marcelo Picanço, CFO of Porto Seguro in Brazil agreed: "Strategy is important, but agile execution is critical – do things fast, identify errors fast and fix them fast."

4. Governance:

As we will argue later, it is very difficult to see how a hybrid could create and retain digital capability without making some major compromises in terms of how their company will adopt the digital organization and how it will operate and integrate with the traditional organization. Such shifts in organization, hierarchy, decision-making, incentivization, motivation, etc. can only be implemented top down.

If the leadership of the hybrid company does not "get it," then it's very unlikely that the digitization of the business can proceed. In terms of management, a new breed needs to be created. The organization has to be populated by people who can deal with ambiguity, who can form and motivate teams, and who can generally operate in a much more fluid environment than is present in most conventional companies. As Robert Philpott, the CEO of Harte Hanks, remarked, "Traditional businesses suffer from the need to get permission to change from their board and shareholders."

The shareholders of these businesses also need to alter behavior by accepting that the traditional objectives of the business will have to be re-calibrated in order to reflect the very different environment implied by the digital landscape. This is a landscape in which speed, flexibility, innovation, the application of technology, obsession with consumer behavior, etc. is paramount. If the digitally-oriented CEO is constantly having to fight his board about the relevance, importance, and complexity of the digital world, and behind them, the shareholders, the right result is unlikely to be delivered. The inspired hybrid has to avoid the trap highlighted by Toon Bouten, CEO of Tomorrow Focus AG: "The board and shareholders of traditional/hybrid businesses can become a major constraint to progress as they often do not understand risk and/or are inherently more conservative."

In terms of rising to these somewhat formidable challenges listed above, the bottom line is that hybrids need to be single-minded about what needs to be achieved in the online part of their business and to "take no hostages" on the way.

For example, it is far better to cannibalize oneself than to cede share. Many traditional businesses have not pursued strategies suited to the digital world as they fear the cannibalization of their existing streams of income. In publishing, this danger is recognized, as this industry was an early victim of the digital age. Michael Hansen, CEO of educational publisher Cengage, observed,

> The resilience of the old educational publishing models was very good as long as it lasted, but if you missed the inflection point you were quickly at risk of survival. The digital world exposed the weaknesses of the

traditional models (lack of user focus and innovation) and rapidly became an important differentiator between those who adopted digital and looked to the future and those who did not.

Winning businesses – both hybrids and pure plays – operate with a mindset that follows the customer opportunity rather than worrying about cannibalization of their own sales.

The insightful hybrids appear to do this through a number of structural mechanisms. For instance, The John Lewis Partnership initially created a discrete unit in order to get started on their digital journey in the early 2000s. They subsequently integrated their digital capability with the mainstream business. At that time John Lewis pioneered the incentivization of store colleagues by crediting them with web sales generated in their own catchment area in order to overcome colleagues' fears of online sales stealing sales from the stores.

"Digital skunkworks can often be the best way of getting started in the online world – progress can be made without interference from 'the traditionalists'," indicated Keith Allen, former COO of Mecom, the Dutch/Danish newspaper publisher.

The good news is that these more inspired approaches have the opposite outcome to the oft-anticipated "zero-sum game." In many cases the size of the pie has been expanded and the hybrids' share in the pie has been increased.

For example, some of the CEOs we interviewed found that when they turned their attention to winning against Amazon, they found themselves gaining share from other weaker multichannel players. This has also resulted in multichannel businesses thinking about how they can distinguish themselves from pure play competitors, e.g. through better supplier relationships, better buying, better customer service, etc.

Another critical factor is pace. As John Walden, the CEO of The Home Retail Group, insisted, "For a traditional company, digital disruption comes from many directions – there are many sources of change and they happen very rapidly – incumbents need to act with urgency and try and imagine what will happen if they do not respond."

And hybrids have many tools at their disposal, if they just thought about it. Sir Martin Sorrell, CEO of media giant WPP, pointed to M&A as a useful tool in the battle between pure plays and hybrids. "The role of acquisitions in the digital era cannot be underestimated. Whether it is 'acqui-hires' designed to recruit talented teams of people or minority stakes to get access to emerging technology, they all have their role."

Perhaps the most difficult challenge for hybrids to overcome is the need to be slightly more ambiguous than deterministic in terms of strategy, product development programs, technology adoption pathways, and the financial consequences of all of the above. This was underlined by Guilherme Loureiro, the President and CEO of Walmart Brazil, who said,

> As you move into a multichannel world, culture becomes critical as the need for greater entrepreneurialism requires you to admit explicitly that your knowledge is less complete than you would like it to be and that you therefore need to tolerate experimentation and failure – arrogance in this arena is the beginning of decline.

We can conclude that hybrids are often slow to understand the new world of "Stractics," where the vision and long-term objectives are clear, but the short- to medium-term way of getting there is somewhat less clear. The fast cycle interaction of consumer behavior, new propositions and fast moving technology militates in favor of a much more empirical approach to strategy and business-model design. Creating the organizations and cultures which allow such "Stractical" approaches to thrive is a nontrivial task, and in the worst cases can give pure plays a "head start" that they do not really deserve.

One European retail CEO we interviewed, Dr Kurt Staelens of Macintosh in the Netherlands, gave a stark warning: "Nowadays online is not a different world – it has to be part of your core business." And this can be difficult for a traditional company to accept, as Mark Hunter, CEO of Molson Coors, observed:

> One of the challenges for hybrids is that organizational capability can lag behind what is required. Senior management can sometimes take time to catch up with what is happening. In this case it becomes important

to be prepared to 'buy the required expertise' and have an internal advocate. Above all, the leadership needs to set the conditions for success.

Antoine de Saint-Affrique, until recently the President of Foods at Unilever, gave hybrids some useful advice: "In order to get the best out of digital, companies need to:

- Raise the floor – for instance, all marketers need to be fluent in digital. The minimum is that you need a digital 'playbook' for each brand/business;
- Raise the ceiling – you need to have some people in the organization who are very ambitious and creative – explorers! Young people who tend to go for the ceiling!
- Reach out – learn from other more nimble organizations about what can be done."

Marjorie Scardino, non-executive director at Twitter and formerly CEO of the global education company Pearson, highlighted the need for clear leadership. When she took over as CEO of Pearson in 1997, she concluded that "Signals are very important. I made sure that continual digital engagement with all the people who worked for me would set the scene that the digital age had come of age."

In closing, we thought we ought to offer hybrids a short checklist against which they can measure themselves:

- Have you created a digital vision about how your company will be even stronger once it does solve the digital conundrum and made digital an integral part of the business model?
- Have you told your digital colleagues to try and maximize the amount of cannibalization that they can inflict on your traditional business?
- Have you persuaded all the "old timers/traditional managers" and "digital disbelievers" that they need to educate themselves and to positively encourage digital insurgency … And that they will be penalized if they "get in the way"?

- Have you made sure that you have got people in your organization who really understand what is going on in the digital world in terms of:
  - Consumer behavior and their interest in, and responses to, digital;
  - What technology now allows you to do, e.g. the power of mobile, or Artificial Intelligence;
  - The necessary skills and capabilities – not to mention organization and culture – without which you will fail in the digital world;
  - Who the emerging competitors are and why they might win;
  - What valuations are attributed to successful digital enterprises?

If you can answer "yes" to these questions, then you are ready for the Stractical world of the successful hybrid.

6

chapter

Pure Plays Versus Hybrids – A Fight to the Finish?

Anyone who generalizes when answering the question of "who will win – pure plays or hybrids?" by answering either hybrids or pure plays is at worst misguided and at best uninformed.

The answer is most certainly "It depends."

What does it depend upon? The first thing that it depends upon is whether the market is susceptible to digital offerings. Here is a checklist which could be used to establish where digital has or will have high relevance:

- The product or the customer interface can be digitized;
- The existing customer experience is inconvenient, slow, uneconomic, or unrewarding;
- Automation will substantially undercut the cost model of the traditional business.

Understanding the second series of factors which impact on whether pure plays or hybrids will win hails back of course to the fundamentals of strategy. You will therefore not be surprised to read that some of the critical factors are relatively simple, as follows:

- Market demand;
- The economics of supply;
- Competitive activity.

Demand: if consumer needs and preferences can be satisfied better digitally, then a fertile market opportunity exists either in terms of creation of a new market or by substituting products and services within an existing one.

Economics of supply: digital economics are so very different versus those in the traditional/physical world. Typically, once you have invested in the systems/applications technology, the cost of serving the incremental customer is low/marginal.

Competitive activity: if barriers to entry are high, then "first-in" often wins in the digital world. Barriers can be intellectual-property driven, the cost of investment/development, or the value of creating and defending pre-emptive/early-market share gains.

If you applied these simple factors to the battle between pure plays and traditional/hybrid companies, you would conclude that pure players should win in some sectors/markets, while traditional/hybrid companies should ultimately win out in others.

We have noted elsewhere that even in sectors where digital clearly has a role, traditional companies nevertheless have three (not so secret) secret weapons:

Brand – When much loved and trusted brands go digital, they can be formidable competitors given that consumers will check out their websites as a matter of preference and be more comfortable giving them personal (including payment) information. Stefan Winners, a board member of Burda Digital Holding, agrees: "Hybrids should believe in the value of their brand – it is a huge barrier to entry to pure play companies and should never be underestimated." The Chairman of Prudential, Paul Manduca, agrees: "Strong brands are critical to digital, particularly in markets where Internet payments are made and trust required."

Buying scale – Which pure plays cannot match, particularly if the hybrid adopts an integrated online/offline strategy (including price) well before the pure play gets to any size/scale.

Supply – The very effective supply chains of important, fast-moving consumer goods companies provide substantial protection. As Jørgen Vig Knudstorp, the CEO of Lego, observed, "Despite the consumer behavior changes in the digital world, one should never underestimate the value of operations. Even now I am sure that our efficient and effective supply chain plays a major role in achieving our superior profitability." In the retail sector, very direct support comes from innovative suppliers who understand that their products need demonstration/explanations/viewing before consumers are likely to adopt them. They are therefore keen to ensure that physical retailers continue to exist to showcase their products.

These examples underpin the belief of Vitor Falleiros, Head of Planning at Brazil's Dafiti, who said, "Pure plays need to be worried about big hybrids – they have the capital, their operational experiences are substantial, and they have great relationships with suppliers."

In markets which are susceptible to digitization, the question therefore is whether traditional/hybrid companies are visionary enough to recognize the potential opportunities created by digitization. These could take a number of forms:

- Products or services that are prone to be digitized, e.g. the physical incarnation of a product is a declining and/or niche part of the market: music, books, photography, gaming, gambling, and news/media qualify on this count.

Products or services where the transactions can be secured through a flow of data: travel bookings, financial services, and event tickets are good examples here.

Products that are physical in nature, but standardized, compact, and require regular replenishment: e.g. printer cartridges and some heavy, commoditized food products.

Products that can be purchased based on the viewing of samples that can be shipped, where home delivery is ultimately required due to their heavy and inconvenient formats. A number of decorating categories are in this category, e.g. paint, wallpaper, and tiling.

The question is then of whether traditional/hybrid companies can move early enough to prevent pure plays from "stealing the march." This is a function of the agility and pace at which the traditional/hybrid company is capable of moving. If their processes and culture are not appropriately aligned, pure plays will have more opportunity.

One example of where a pure play appears to be winning (even versus other pure plays) is the US legal market, i.e. helping businesses and consumers find a lawyer when they need one – often very quickly!

How did Americans find lawyers in "the old days"?

Let's assume you had a non-fatal car crash and you needed to get a lawyer to take up your claim for compensation against either your, or the other driver's, insurance company. In the old paper-based days you would probably go home, talk to a friend who may know a lawyer or at least know about lawyers or alternatively pick up your phone directory (remember them?) and look up "Lawyers." You would then put a pin in the list and make a phone call. Alternatively, if you were a US businessman looking for lawyers, you would probably reach for a copy of *Martindale Hubbell*, a massive tome which listed all lawyers in the US with their specializations and rated them. This was published and updated a number of times a year so it reflected, roughly, who was in the market.

So how is Avvo transforming this market?

Avvo estimates that there are some 0.6 million active lawyers in the US. They currently have approximately a third of these lawyers signed up on their service. Let's go back to our non-fatal car crash. At the site of the crash you probably already know that you're going to need a lawyer. By signing up to the Avvo service, you can immediately report the circumstances of your need and expect to be phoned back by a relevant and competent local (as far as possible) lawyer within 15 minutes. You could even transmit the pictures of the crash to the lawyer, who will advise you how to proceed.

The lawyers are vetted and rated by Avvo so that you know what you're getting. Increasingly, ambitious lawyers are not only signing up to their site but also making themselves available out of hours. Prices are transparent and in some cases taken from a menu of services, so that you know where you are.

This service has many transformational characteristics:

- Immediacy
- Convenience
- Relevance
- Security/confidence
- Affordability/transparency
- Full customization for mobile

There are other online lawyer services, but their reach both in terms of customers and lawyers is much more modest thanks to the speed with which Avvo has recruited lawyers and marketed its services to customers. Avvo is delivering in terms of a unique proposition and is rewarded by high growth and a suitably impressive valuation. Having taken early market share they will be very difficult for a follower to compete with.

There are equally strong examples where pure plays have started the ball rolling, but incumbents (traditional/hybrid companies) will demonstrate, or have already demonstrated, that they can rule the day. For instance, consumer retail banking has long been a low/no touch business for many customers.

Pre-Internet banking, one wrote checks and received printed bank statements in the mail. You had to go down to the local branch of the bank to get cash, pay bills or transfer money but it was often an unrewarding experience. You were greeted by an uninspiring cashier having waited in a queue for at least ten minutes.

The attraction of never having to go into a branch bank again is therefore huge.

It was hardly surprising therefore, when "no touch, telephone banking" by a telephone banking operation, First Direct, launched it was very successful. Indeed, in terms of customer service, branch-free banks have been very successful.

First Direct (now owned by HSBC) was ranked top in a recent UK survey run by the very well-respected consumer watchdog, *Which?*, who surveyed some 3,621 consumers, asking them which brands were customer service champions and which were not up to scratch. First Direct's stellar rating of 87% put to shame the ratings of the major banks (NatWest, Santander, HSBC, the Royal Bank of Scotland, Barclays), who could only muster ratings of 70–71%, far behind First Direct.

Since then there have been some Internet-only banking entrants into the UK banking market, not least Egg, and ING Direct (the latter, interestingly, owned by a non-UK bank who wished to enter the UK, but without opening branches). Both of these entrants are now owned by traditional UK banks – Barclays and Yorkshire Building Society respectively. They were late to the game but the role of Internet banking in the UK is now undisputed and complements other branch-free banking services, such as automatic cash dispensers and online account querying/money transfer capabilities. By supporting these services with outstanding and well-informed telephone customer services the industry is being transformed. Indeed, checks are now being phased out, as are printed bank statements, given that many millions of customers are now signing up for online-only banking.

The consumer utility of online banking is clear – paying bills and checking your accounts can be done at any time of the day with minimum fuss and no brisk walks down to the post box to mail your instructions to your bank.

Interestingly, the early moves into online banking were undertaken by pure plays, but as soon as the threat became clear the traditional companies moved in and used their brands and distribution capabilities to maintain market share.

The UK retail market can also offer up examples of where hybrids can hold their own despite the onslaught of Amazon and other pure play distribution alternatives.

In the same *Which?* survey to which we referred earlier in this chapter, John Lewis (a UK department store) was number three.

John Lewis is a hybrid business, and a very successful one too, with high ratings both for their in-store and for their online experiences. Indeed John Lewis received the OmniChannel Retailer of the Year award at the 2014 World Retail Congress, beating a multitude of impressive international competitors.

What has made them able to resist the onslaught of pure play propositions such as AO.com and Amazon?

In a phrase: Commitment to a multichannel vision and future … and a culture which can deliver it.

John Lewis has consistently fostered an impressive multichannel ethos by:

- Giving targets to shop branch managers on online catchment sales as well as store based sales.
- Ensuring managers on the shop floor are also incentivized on any in-store assisted, online purchases which their department makes.
- Investing in integrated customer support systems, creating a "one view" of customer orders and a single supply chain across channels.

Customers, in the meantime, get the best of both worlds. They can view a furniture range in-store and then decide in the comfort of their own homes whether to order it, what finishes to choose, and when to have it delivered, by ordering it online at their leisure, e.g. late at night when stores are not open. By pursuing this multichannel purchasing behavior they gain confidence in their purchase, as well as the convenience of online shopping, all in a single package.

The story in consumer electronics is similar but importantly different. A 42-inch Brand LED TV (Code HPS42THEBEST) is the same if bought in-store or online. So will people not always buy it online? They would instantly know whether it is in stock and at what price, and it can be delivered at their convenience.

Again, the answer is "it depends."

And it largely depends on:

- Is the product new and stuffed full of features which are complicated to understand?
- Does it confusingly sound exactly like a similar model from another manufacturer e.g. Samsung, Philips, Sony, Panasonic, etc.?
- Will the people in-store match the online price/delivery/convenience offered by the pure play?
- Are the pure play retailers in this space ones who I would trust with my personal (payment) details, and will they vouch for the product's authenticity?

If the answer to the first three of these questions is "yes" and the fourth one is "no" or "not sure," then a trip to your local Dixons, Darty, or BestBuy is probably warranted. All three of these "complex electronics" retailers are aggressively positioned against pure plays as they:

- Have their own online home delivery offerings.
- Have staff who know the products and can advise you on the one best suited to your needs.
- Have attractive prices both offline and online.

We have argued above that pure plays can sometimes win and that sometimes hybrids can successfully defend their marketplaces against pure plays. For completeness we should also note that there are sectors which may continue to be traditional for some time, although probably not for ever.

These sectors often display one or other of the following characteristics:

- Where technology has yet to be developed to a level which permits the physical to be substituted by digital, as in the case of eye tests in the optical value chain, or equipment-fitting in golf.
- Where purchase frequency is low and word-of-mouth and inertia mean incumbents continue to remain in business, e.g. tradesmen in

the home improvement sector, which explains why models such as Angie's List in the US and Rated People in the UK have not genuinely scaled up.

- Where the purchase risk (including payment information) is perceived to be high, e.g. cars. Here brands can play a critical role especially because the rate of innovation is high, and comparison between competing products is complicated and non-obvious. In these cases, advice from sales staff is important, versus reading lots of technical specifications on websites.

In closing, we note that we might be accused of having too tight definitions in terms of pure plays versus hybrids.

Implicitly, we have assumed that the differences between pure plays and hybrids are dramatic, distinct, and enduring. However, increasingly, businesses operating in the digital world often do not display such clear cut differences. Many businesses which are considered to be pure plays actually duplicate some of the higher cost features of hybrids.

For instance, AO.com, a very recent and highly valued listing on the UK stock market, has a substantial supply chain in order to get its white-goods products from manufacturers to customers. In addition, they have significant customer service costs, partly mirroring the cost that their hybrid competitors have in running physical stores.

Similarly, hybrids have set up very slick online operations which reflect many of the efficiencies and creativity of their pure play competitors. For instance, major UK grocers pioneered the "Store Pick" model for online grocery delivery, thereby reducing the capital intensity of the picking operations and cost of delivery to customers.

Regrettably, however, hybrids do not uniformly demonstrate the capability to implement this relatively straightforward parallel tracking of their traditional and digital businesses. We address this elsewhere in this book, but suffice it to say that it is indeed a visionary hybrid leadership that recognizes the need to go digital early and creates the correct organizational and cultural framework for it to happen with minimum fuss and without it being crushed by the overbearing processes and disciplines of the mother ship of the traditional business.

Asmita Dubey of L'Oréal underlined the importance of leadership when she said,

> It's almost impossible to succeed unless your leadership believes in digital and is relatively hands-on with respect to how the online journey is being undertaken. They need to set the ambition, learn how to educate the traditionalists, and what sort of risks are acceptable. They also need to ensure that the right talent is brought into the company in a structure which will allow it to succeed.

This means that we can now predict with a degree of confidence that some sectors will probably be relatively immune from domination by pure plays, while others are going to migrate steadfastly in the direction of online-only services. Traditional companies or hybrids who are already competing in these sectors either need to transform themselves very rapidly or contemplate winding their businesses down in a way that best optimizes cash flow in the time they have left.

We hope, therefore, that we have demonstrated why there is no generalized answer to the question "who is likely to win, pure play or hybrid?"

This is further complicated by the fact that national boundaries do play a role. The outcome of which model, pure play or hybrid, succeeds is also determined by the country/region in which it operates.

Where dispersed but digitally savvy populations exist (China) and the cost of rolling out traditional retail models is high, pure play retailers will succeed, whereas this might not be the case for the same retail sector in the UK. This is certainly a factor in the exponential growth of Yihaodian and Alibaba in China. The same conditions do not pertain in, for example, Turkey or India, where there is a more stable coexistence of hybrid and pure play solutions.

But the overall message is clear. As one European retail CEO, Dr Kurt Staelens of the Dutch retailer, Macintosh, correctly noted, "Hybrids can have many advantages, e.g. a massive customer base which pure plays have to build, physical assets which can be used to create multichannel loyalty, e.g. in-store demonstrations, in-store advice/maintenance etc." In these cases, pure plays will have an uphill battle.

To demonstrate the unpredictability of category penetration versus country penetration, Figure 6.1 might be instructive. While there are only six categories which globally have more than 15% online penetration, many individual countries identify more than six categories with more than 15% penetration in their country. We conclude that national context and consumer behavior are thus all-important, and that generalizations could be dangerous.

In summary, pure plays will probably not end up ruling the world. There is a place for both models, depending on the characteristics of the sector and the technological maturity of the market.

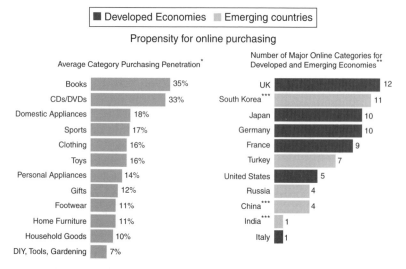

There is a place for both models, depending on the characteristics of the sector

FIGURE 6.1 **Propensity for online purchasing**

Note: *Average across Top 25 E-commerce markets, categories with >15% of internet users who have made an online purchase in this category.
**Number of categories with penetration >15%.
***OC&C estimates based on Spend per Connected for India and South Korea. China from CNIC.

In this vein, some good advice for hybrids was given by Yu Gang, co-founder and Chairman of Yihaodian, a pure play, when he said, "What hybrids have to do is:

- commit to winning not 'playing';
- empower the online units;
- focus on customers instead of competitors by:
- fully leverage the synergies of the online and offline resources;
- have outstanding logistics;
- deliver excellent sales support;
- recruit online people with e-commerce genes;
- reward cannibalization and digital success."

If you follow this advice and are in a sector where hybrids can hold their own (or are the winning model), then you should have little to fear from pure plays.

chapter 7

The Principles Underpinning Success in the World of Stractics

The road to "Stractical" success is strewn with obstacles, challenges, and pitfalls. Success for either pure plays or hybrids is by no means guaranteed.

Nevertheless, we have been able to identify a number of principles which should prevent companies falling into the deepest potholes on the road to success. Interestingly we would recommend these principles to both hybrids and pure plays. Both seek to succeed in the new world of Stractics. By paying attention to the principles below, we feel their chances are improved.

we would recommend these principles to both hybrids and pure plays

Needless to say, there had to be 10 principles, and here they are:

1. Start with vision and purpose.
2. Be obsessed by customers and consumers and their behavior.
3. Embed the right planning horizons.
4. Understand and invest in competitive differentiation and advantage – innovate, innovate, innovate!
5. Harness technology effectively.
6. Build a robust business model which encompasses an ecosystem of staff, suppliers, customers, etc.
7. Do not tolerate mediocrity.

8. Reinvent yourself frequently.
9. Design a new governance model.
10. Build a fit-for-purpose organization with an agile culture.

For the reader of the first six chapters of this book, we suspect that these principles are by now no surprise. Operating successfully (and "stractically") in the digital world is not straightforward, but on the other hand it's also not impossible. A key first step is to recognize the very fundamental differences between the conventional and the digital world, and which of those differences need to be reflected in your approach to managing the business.

Start with vision and purpose

In a business landscape where so much is in flux and new ways of operating are constantly being developed, never before has the need for an inspiring vision and audacious goals been greater. Such visions have a dramatic effect on the ability of companies to attract, in equal measure people and finance.

These goals can be couched in financial or non-financial terms. Whichever type of goal is chosen, organizations should focus on statements of intent that help create a sense of ambition and purpose.

For example, Moneysupermarket.com oriented itself around saving UK consumers £1billion in 2012, which translates into 500,000 households saving £200 each. This created an organization motivated by helping people save money. Its CEO, Peter Plumb, said, "If you focus on Revenue/ EBIT (earnings before interest and taxes), you lose focus on the goals which the customer values."

Sample vision statements

Amazon "Be Earth's most customer-centric company"	**Tripadvisor** "Help people around the world plan and have the perfect trip"
Facebook "Give people the power to share and make the world more open and connected"	**Google** "Organise the world's information and make it universally accessible and useful"

Continued

LinkedIn "Connect the world's professionals to make them more productive and successful"	**Netflix** "Become the best global entertainment distribution service"
eBay "Provide a global online marketplace where practically anyone can trade practically anything enabling economic opportunity around the world"	**Expedia** "Own and power the best travel brands in the world"

Be obsessed by customers and consumers and their behavior

The competitive battleground in digital businesses is clearly for the hearts and minds of the consumer. Unless you can command very large numbers of customers and preferably very high market shares you gain only relatively modest recognition in the digital world. As Peter Plumb, CEO of Moneysupermarket.com said, "You have to put yourself in the seat of the consumer." Matt Brittin, VP of Google Europe, agrees: "The business model needs to replicate the customer journey." L'Oréal's Asmita Dubey confirmed this when she said, "In the online world hybrids have to revisit and understand the customer journey," as did Pepsi's Anne Tse, who said, "You always need to go through the customer journey if you want to know where digital enhances the experience."

A simple way of demonstrating these differences can be seen in Figure 7.1. Here, we analyzed the 10K reports/the Chairman's letters of two leading pure play companies and compared the most frequently used words with those of two leading traditional/hybrid companies. In the pure plays, the words "customer," "user," "services," "products," and "information" dominate. For the hybrids, "stores," "retail," "fast expansion," and "merchandise" dominate. A subtle but critical difference in attitudes and perspectives.

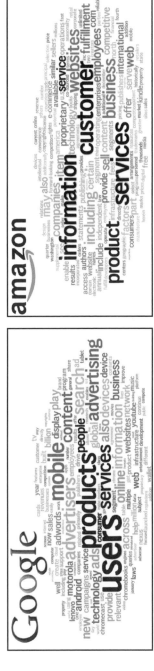

FIGURE 7.1 / Key word associations of pure play and hybrid brands

This emphasis on customers/users has been underlined by such pure play visionaries as John Roberts, the CEO of AO.com in the UK, one of the most successful modern initial public offerings (IPOs) in the digital space: "The web hasn't changed what customers want, it has empowered them. We want to consistently be the best in how we treat our customers."

In terms of consumers, there are three major issues which should preoccupy digital players:

1. **Engagement/acquisition.** Sometimes the online proposition is sufficiently compelling that customer acquisition deals with itself. Facebook never had to spend a great deal of money acquiring consumers. Its reputation spread virally and by word of mouth, meaning that it reached hundreds of millions of consumers with very modest marketing spend. For less inspiring and more functional online propositions, more creative ways of acquiring customers need to be thought through. Often these would involve "pay per click" investments or the purchase of massive customer databases. One way or the other, you have to make these investments early in order to "make the market" and then take a substantial share of it.

2. **Customer service.** The key attribute of good customer service is rapid and satisfactory resolution of the customer issue at low levels of customer effort. By resolving such issues "first-time", costs and customer dissatisfaction are reduced…which can also help with retention / loyalty, which we deal with next.

3. **Retention/loyalty.** Creating a consumer franchise and a loyal customer base is of course Nirvana. Not only does this bring consumers back but it also means they are probably telling all their friends and neighbors about you too. It also means that you can begin to track long-term customer behavior, which will allow you increasingly to refine your proposition and make it more and more attractive and relevant. This will give shoppers every incentive to shop repeatedly thereby increasing the lifetime value of a customer. Funders and investors will reward you handsomely for creating and benefiting from the virtuous

circle of a loyal customer base. "Loyal customers are gold dust," observed Peter Plumb of Moneysupermarket.com.

While these consumer-oriented principles are probably self-evident, how to execute them may not be. In the digital world, many of the techniques related to accessing, serving, and retaining consumers involve data. Whether it is communicating with customers in the first place, or analyzing their purchasing/shopping behavior, data is at the epicenter of all things digital.

In terms of data, the advice from our interviewees was consistently the same:

> **Collect it** – do not avoid it! Indeed Peter Plumb, CEO of Moneysupermarket.com, advised: "Collect it first and foremost and worry later about what you do with it." It is important to build a culture where the entire organization tracks key metrics on a frequent (even hourly) basis and uses it to define their next actions. "Where the metrics are deviating from what we expect, the entire organization is able to manage by exception and we isolate and address performance issues rapidly," said the CEO of an Indian pure play.

> **Use it to co-create** – understanding customers is not only about the pure statistical data but also about qualitative real-time customer feedback data. By using this customer information propositions can be delivered / refined continuously to make them keep in tune with the market. "Being data-driven is about keeping in touch with customer reactions at all times. In the world of physical branches, it was always very difficult for everyone to get access to customer data. In the digital world everyone can see this in real time," reports a banking executive.

> This view was very much reinforced by Sachin Bansal, the CEO of Flipkart, when he said, "After every order, we ask customers for their feedback and ten to 15% of them respond. At any given point in time, at least 50% of the business is working on improvements that are the result of this feedback. For example, we spotted a consistent drop in our customer satisfaction/NPS ratings in the city of Hyderabad and an

investigation of the root cause highlighted negative feedback on packaging, which we were able to improve rapidly."

An even greater endorsement of co-creation came from S. Sivakumar, Divisional CEO of Agri and IT businesses at India's ITC Agribusiness, who stated: "All the consumers who participate in our digital media and call centre channels become part of the qualitative research and thereby become co-creators for the best flavors, range, and value that we can introduce into our products."

Social media also play an important part in terms of brand health and brand sales, because they can provide very good early warning signals about how consumers are thinking about brands. Krishan Ganesh, CEO of Big Basket, said:

Social media keeps us on our toes all the time – the viral nature of the customers' reactions and fast response times means that we are a 24/7 business. Thanks to social media, we have been able to launch products far more quickly, with greater proof on their ability to scale.

However, data does not answer all questions. For instance, Nevzat Aydin, the CEO of Yemeksepeti in Turkey, indicated that "being customer centric clearly matters. However, you need to be 'customer ahead'. In other words you need to know what customers want even before they know it themselves."

Many pure plays find that being customer obsessed comes easily, as Eduardo Baek, a founder of the leading Brazilian online optical company eÓtica observed: "Pure plays tend to be less worried about competitors and more worried about how to bring offline customers into the online world."

Embed the Right Planning Horizons

If you talk to any pure plays you will immediately conclude that they have a vision of what they are trying to achieve but, as we have noted above, seldom do they have detailed plans about how they are going to get there.

- "We cannot have a five-year strategy in the digital world as the planning assumptions will change substantially over that time period. Strategic timelines in our world are much shorter. Nevertheless we need to work towards one big longer-term vision of becoming 'the biggest retailer in Turkey'," said Emre Ekmekçi, Head of Business Development at Hepsiburada, one of Turkey's leading retailers.
- "In the old era, you could make a three-year plan and stick to it. If we ever execute our three-year plan precisely as we conceived it, something has gone wrong and we have failed. You need to have one, to provide a basis for planning office space, incentive plans, and bank facilities, but you need to be dynamic in evolving it too. This is not to say our strategy constantly changes – our three big strategic priorities still remain the same as they were three, or even ten years ago, but it is the execution that changes and evolves," said Tim Steiner, CEO of Ocado.
- "We have a three-year plan, but we also realise that we need to be constantly attentive," agreed Andy Street, MD of The John Lewis Partnership.

The absence of a three-year plan does not make digital companies strategically weak, however. More importantly, embedding the right planning timescales into your business model is a critical element of your ultimate success.

Similarly, where companies do have a three-year plan it does not mean, as long as their philosophy is digitally attuned, that their thinking is flawed, as observed by Peter Plumb, the CEO of Moneysupermarket.com:

> The three-year plan has still not gone out of favour, necessarily. Some CEOs still see it as a useful planning tool, although the key difference is that in the traditional world, an ambitious plan would require you to double in three years; in the digital world, doubling is the planning

assumption for six months. The levels of ambition with which plans are underpinned are fundamentally different.

Given that the digital world and its underpinning technology is developing so fast, it is entirely defensible to have a business model that is experimental and empirical. As part of that business model, extremely rapid feedback loops allow you to refine and develop your customer proposition, your understanding of how customers behave, the challenges for the supply chain and how, ultimately, you might make money. All of these are critical elements of a successful business model.

It is therefore critical to build the organization and its "thinking" processes accordingly. Inevitably, in the digital world this requires far more frequent staging points and milestones. For instance, Matt Brittin, VP of Google Northern and Central Europe, noted: "The normal three- to five-year strategy plan would be redundant the moment you wrote it. However, assessing top to bottom objectives and key results every quarter gives us the ability to stay focused and also to pivot where we see greater opportunity." Sachin Bansal, CEO of Flipkart agreed: "The planning rhythm that works best for our business is to have an annual operating plan, and every quarter we typically update or add two to three strategic initiatives based on how we see the market and technology evolve."

This does of course create problems for hybrids, who are somewhat constrained by the need to have strategies, plans and budgets. The relatively fast-changing digital world can create budget chaos. Unfortunately, in the digital world you sometimes just have to swallow hard and accept that the budget is a useful tool for planning horizons, but not an inflexible one and cast in stone. This was reinforced by Nevzat Aydin, the CEO of Yemeksepeti:

> If you ask me what my budget for next year is, I would say, "I don't know." To succeed, budgets need to be flexible because decisions can now be made faster, with better data, at the point in time where it improves the decision rather than a year in advance. Our agile approach to decision making and budgeting helps us compete.

Understand and invest in competitive differentiation and advantage

In the digital world, competitive differentiation/ advantage can be made up of a combination of a number of things, such as a low-cost business model, the proposition/brand itself, unique technology, a very efficient supply chain, and other factors, such as the rate of innovation and even brand strength.

competitive differentiation/advantage can be made up of a number of a combination of things

Whatever you believe are the sources of competitive advantage, you need to be very honest and self-critical in order to make sure that the advantage is truly valid, and applicable to the marketplace in which you compete.

In terms of the individual sources of competitive advantage, we show below some examples of how they need to work.

Sebastian James, the Group Chief Executive of Dixons Carphone, highlighted the need for hybrids to be particularly vigilant on costs: "Multichannel players need to be clear about how they can compete with the cost structure of a pure play – it is critical to understand the total value chain economics of a pure play as well as your own hybrid model." We would observe, however, that sometimes it is a myth that pure plays have a low cost base, given that their back office can sometimes be similar to a hybrid but potentially less well managed!

Brand-building in the digital world is possibly even more critical than in the traditional marketplaces. Brands pull people to your website/ Facebook page and, hopefully, make them loyal. This is non-trivial because "staying front of mind is an expensive business for a pure play," said the CEO of a major British retailer. "Digital marketing is useful for introductions and trials but tends not to be sustainable long term as it is so expensive. It is more important to focus on how you go from visitor to customer, which is often a reflection of the quality and depth of your brand," added Peter Plumb of Moneysupermarket.com.

Often, technology plays an enormous role, as confirmed by Tim Steiner, the CEO of Ocado, when he said, "We see ourselves as a technology business as much as we see ourselves as a retail business. Our competitors only *use* technology, whereas we develop it! We don't use other people's software – we believe in doing it ourselves and hence it has become a core competence."

In terms of the supply chain, it was noted by Jean-Christophe Garbino, the CEO of Kiabi, that "the key component of a good digital business is its supply chain. You need to build a specific supply chain benchmarking best practice seen in low-cost pure play models."

In the new world of Stractics, the importance of innovation cannot be underestimated. Given that the competitive landscape is changing so fast and so frequently, embedding innovation as a core part of the business model is critical. If you don't, you risk becoming a digital dinosaur quite quickly. Google is very conscious of this risk, as its Northern and Central European VP, Matt Brittin pointed out: "Watch out for someone small and innovative who could make you irrelevant."

embedding innovation as a core part of the business model is critical

> You have to notice the signs for when the tide is turning and to reflect that in your priorities. For instance, we were at the forefront of spotting the mobile opportunity and prioritizing efforts to get the first mobile app out. Today we do 45% of our business on the mobile and we are already thinking about how smart watches can be used to make it even easier for our customers to shop at Ocado,

said Tim Steiner, CEO of Ocado. He went on to say, "We are not constrained by ideas – we've got so many. We are constrained by the capability to execute them technologically."

In short, innovation is the critical lifeblood of an organization, and determines success in the digital world. Gavin Patterson, CEO of BT, reinforced this when he recommended that, "Innovation should not be separated from the core business. It should be ingrained in the business, celebrated more, and talked about so that the correct behaviors can be encouraged, particularly when times are tough and the general environment may not be conducive to risk-taking."

Jørgen Vig Knudstorp, CEO of Denmark's Lego Worldwide, went further when he indicated that in and of itself innovation might not always be enough,

> You cannot be complacent in the digital world. Indeed we are currently going through a process which, despite our success to date in the digital world, will allow us to reinvent ourselves once again by making sure that technology is in the heart of our business and that by not waiting for "a burning platform" we can invest ahead of the market with the right people and the right propositions.

Irrespective of how you are innovating or reinventing, a good test for whether you're succeeding in terms of the creation of competitive differentiation and/or advantage was defined by Andy Street, MD of The John Lewis Partnership, when he said, "Focus on beating the best, even if they are not your most direct competitors, because it makes you stronger."

Harness Technology Effectively

Do not make the mistake of believing that "IT" is the same as "digital technology." The sort of technology that makes digital businesses work is not the same as the information technology (IT) that is at the core of many traditional businesses. It is very much more consumer-oriented and is as much about consumer interface as it is around transaction or supply chain management. In fact it should be called CT: customer or consumer technology.

"To succeed in the digital world, businesses need new information architects, a different breed of technology people who are able to build applications and more complex data structures. Identifying those architects is what corporates should focus on," opined Florian Heinemann of Project A. Marjorie Scardino, NED at Twitter and former CEO at global education company Pearson, confirmed, "There may be a conflict between CTOs who prefer working on big enterprise systems and bespoke projects with multi-year deadlines and those who would rely on software services and modular solutions that can be developed faster and are better suited to the propositions and demands that change rapidly and unpredictably in business."

In addition, new technologies need to focus on the "front end" of many business models, not on the "back office," as IT used to do.

ITC's S. Sivakumar reported that: "At the consumer end we still need to do more to capitalize on faster consumers' feedback. This will improve our existing products and help us launch new ones. The ultimate Nirvana will be when we can e-enable all our customers."

A particular message for hybrids is that "the cost of poor or slow technology is very high," said Prashant Tandon of HealthKart. This was reinforced by Professor Annet Aris of INSEAD, who said: "One of the major challenges for incumbents is that they find it very difficult to bridge the data and technology gap. The gap between the theoretical opportunities they face and their ability to do something about them is vast."

Sachin Bansal, the founder of Flipkart, also remarked on the importance of agility in order to make the most of technology developments:

> Agility is very important – you cannot be married to a thought process for too long. Three years ago, we could not have foreseen what we are doing. The smartphone used to be a premium product but today it is a commodity in everyone's hands. Our fleet drivers all bring their own device and we have been able to develop applications for smart routing that work on their devices making it possible for us to operate our fleet better than we had ever thought we would be able to. It is difficult to predict the pace of technology innovation, so we need to be flexible to adapt our strategy as new innovations gain ground.

Build a Robust Business Model which Encompasses an Ecosystem of Staff, Suppliers, and Customers

In the early years of the digital era, hybrids usually put their e-commerce/online teams in a separate organizational entity so as to ...

- not pollute the mainstream with radical and often disruptive ideas;
- not allow the mainstream to smother the new ideas about how to compete in the digital world.

At the same time, pure plays were outstanding in terms of understanding front-end consumer interface issues, but were sometimes naïvely incompetent with respect to the management of fulfilment and the supply chain.

Nowadays, both pure plays and hybrids understand the need to have a fully integrated business model. By engaging with consumers in co-creation, getting suppliers to provide inventory (and even delivery systems), and making sure your own organization is capable of optimizing across a multichannel consumer engagement model, it is critical to integrate the digital assets of a business with its physical assets. Moving from a decentralized model to a fully integrated model is not without its challenges, mostly related to people, which are dealt with elsewhere in this chapter.

it is critical to integrate the digital assets of a business with its physical assets

For the meantime, let's just reinforce the need for integration from a few messages from our interviewees ...

1. **Consumers.** "You have to be fully integrated between all channels – one brand, one customer, one goal, and have to be very good in social networking and address all the channels effectively. It is easy to have fans but you need more than 'fans' or 'likes,' you need people interacting, participating, talking about the brand and from fans to community. It takes two to three right individuals in a small team focused on getting all these social media channels to work – it's not a numbers game, but a game of skill." (Jean-Christophe Garbino, CEO, Kiabi)

2. **Suppliers.** "We work with our supplier base in a collaborative way and give them access to our assets and capabilities in order to grow their business. This mainly takes two forms – firstly, we run tactical programs to help them improve traffic to their products which also enables onsite monetization for us; secondly, we give them analytics support on the overall category, key trends and recommendations for new products they might want to launch, new price points that they might want to consider introducing and other levers to grow their business with us." (Sachin Bansal, CEO, Flipkart)

3. **People/organization.** "Cross-functional is key: It is very difficult in today's world to divide every process of such an organization into a single function. We are all connected. For instance, it's not possible to improve the digital marketing without the IT efforts. We discuss our group's strategy with the cross functional team, so when an idea is not aligned with the company strategy, people are able to challenge each other. We are making the strategy and pipeline visible to everybody." (Ilker Baydar, CEO, Markafoni)

Do Not Tolerate Mediocrity

As noted in our previous book, *Making Your Strategy Work*, why would you expect a great strategy to be implemented by mediocre people? Robert Philpott, CEO of Harte Hanks, agreed; "The strategic issue is always people."

In the digital world, therefore, the quality of your people and the culture in which they operate can translate into a massive competitive advantage. In the digital world creating a culture of openness so that even the most junior people can influence the direction of the business makes all the difference. In the digital world, insight and creativity is not necessarily correlated with experience.

In addition, team working is at a premium, as John Roberts, the CEO of AO.com, confirmed: "The operational gearing of ten great people working together is immense and very humbling." In addition he noted:

> My number one preoccupation in the medium term is on getting the right quality of individuals into the business and focusing on how they

work together. In addition, many organizations tend to recruit by role but we have a team of four recruiters who are constantly recruiting not for role, but for talent. A focus on identifying brilliant people with the right culture and DNA means that when we need to scale, we can scale quickly.

Pure plays translate this into true competitive advantage by organizing to get the most out of a talented workforce who are used to building at speed. Small teams focused on tough problems can make rapid inroads – an all-important characteristic for success in the digital world! As Peter Plumb of Moneysupermarket.com observed, "People are the critical issue when scaling up. We could double our sales by adding 150 people [approximately 25% of the current headcount] to our workforce. They just have to be the right 150!"

This is a world where excellence and attitude trump experience, as evidenced by some of our CEO interviews:

- Mark Britton, Founder of the online lawyer business Avvo in the US, remarked: "Technology is moving very fast at the cutting edge of online. For instance, mobile is key and is becoming more important. Being able to search using marked up content when you are on the move is critical. If you can't get hold of the right technological guru in these particular technologies you are going to be at a disadvantage."
- "My number one mid long-term focus is on the quality of individuals in the business and how they work together" (John Roberts, CEO, AO.com)
- "We are comfortable hiring less experienced talent just for their potential. In various ways, experience has lost value in the digital world. We hire young people often in their first job and give them lots of responsibility. However, you also need the know-how of experienced professionals. The right mix of senior experts and young talent will be key for a team's success and culture" (Florian Heinemann, Founder, Project A)
- "Experience is overrated – young generalists who are ready to take on challenges make the biggest impact in the organization," Nevzat Aydin, CEO of Yemeksepeti.

- If you can't hire the talent, you sometimes have to buy it through small deals. "We have made many small acquisitions, often 'acqui-hires,' to help us get new capabilities and new blood," admits Matt Brittin, the VP of Google's Northern and Central European operations.

It would be wrong to leave this section without mentioning succession – a profound issue for many pure plays where the founding entrepreneur was great at starting the enterprise but who may be less good or even, at worst, disastrous at scaling it up. This issue needs to be addressed head-on. Some entrepreneurs are just not good at building and managing infrastructure which is often at the heart of the larger and more successful pure plays.

One of our interviewees, José Rogério Luiz, VP of Planning at Netshoes in Brazil, noted that

> Entrepreneurs are good at creating and growing companies but not so good when they get large – their attitude is often "planning is for losers," which is often a failing strategy. Pure plays grow big and the people find themselves employed in surprisingly large companies – the biggest in which they have ever worked and for which they are ill-suited in some cases. In these circumstances they should hand over to experienced managers.

By avoiding the succession issue investors and staff may be massively unrewarded.

Reinvent Yourself Frequently

One of the truisms of the digital world is, of course, that nothing stands still for very long. Hybrids in particular find the need to reinvent themselves a big challenge. "Incumbents (hybrids) are still lagging – the age of their management teams and their fear of cannibalization are major hurdles for them. In addition, most are not succeeding in reinventing themselves but merely continue to pursue their traditional (and very complex) processes and systems," opined Frederik Nieuwenhuys, a serial digital entrepreneur from the Netherlands.

In line with these comments, it is incumbent upon the leadership of any business affected by the digital economy to make sure that management is constantly benchmarking itself as to whether its business continues to be fit for purpose and is responding to customer and competitive requirements. If not, it needs to reinvent itself rapidly in order to ensure its long-term existence. You only have to think of the experience of Nokia, who ignored the onslaught of the smart phone (which enabled consumers to interact with the Internet and the digital world on the move) to be convinced that failure is the only outcome of digital corporate indolence, overconfidence or ignorance.

> You need to be willing to disrupt yourself, which is something that large organizations naturally find hard to do. For instance, we spent the first six years building a business that works well in a desktop world, but we have had to reverse that entirely and orient ourselves around the mobile world which has been a painful shift for us. The customer opportunity in mobile is very different to what we were used to in the desktop world – because your mobile (smart) phone is always with you, visits and purchases are less pre-meditated, the screen size changes how you aid discoverability; and you have ten times more data to aid decision-making. This shift has therefore been a profound one for us and a key driver of our continued growth. (Sachin Bansal, CEO, Flipkart)

"It is important to keep your eye on the next wave of growth and how the business model is likely to evolve. As the CEO, that is the number one priority I spend my time on," said Nevzat Aydin, CEO of Yemeksepeti. "However, if you do this well then it can be very powerful."

Andrew Crawley, Chief Commercial Officer of British Airways, gave an excellent example of successful reinvention:

> Nowadays we do not only think of BA as an airline. Competition is often not other airlines but booking systems such as Expedia etc. We therefore also think of ourselves as a retailer. In this vein our content (flight schedules etc.) is massively valuable, as is that of our partners.

Design a new governance model including

1. **Shareholders with long-term conviction.** Without doubt, pure plays have the advantage here, given that their money is inherently seeking huge reward but on the understanding that it can only be achieved by taking substantial risk. Pension funds and more conservative investors who are usually to be found on the boards of hybrids are less tolerant of risk and often do not understand the concept of learning through failure – an important aspect of the digital world.

2. **An informed board.** Again, pure plays have boards who tend to be made up of people with experience or understanding of the rules of the digital game. They are aware of the inherent risk of operating in the digital world and the need for rapid and empirical progress. Hybrids need to face up to this challenge, as confirmed by Paul Manduca, Chairman of Prudential, who stated that: "Boards need to understand the impact of digital. It is inconceivable that modern corporations, when dealing with consumers, can avoid playing in the digital world."

   Hybrids have a more fundamental issue given that they have to persuade a board which tends to be made up of relatively conventional leaders whose major experience lies outside the digital landscape. An insightful management team will tend to make sure that their board members have the opportunity to educate themselves in the appropriate digital curriculum and/or persuade the Chairman to make sure that the board has a mix of digitally competent individuals complementing the capabilities of more conventional board members. The CEO of a prominent UK retail group had some clear advice: "The board and shareholders need to understand the changes that need to be made and how the inherent risk profile changes. You need to educate them and possibly even add a few individuals who 'get it' and help you mobilize support around the multichannel vision." Dr Rainer Hillebrand of Otto confirmed this: "The rapid pace of the digital world requires the board (and behind them the shareholders) to control the business more frequently and make sure that actions are being taken as a consequence."

3. **An inspired leadership**. As noted elsewhere, the behavior of the CEO sends out hugely important messages to the rest of the organization about the importance of digital and the way in which the organization needs to embrace online opportunities:

    i. "The role of the CEO can never be underestimated. His or her behavior will determine whether the organization takes digital seriously or not. We do!" said Mark Hunter, the CEO of Molson Coors. Marcelo Picanço, CFO at Porto Seguro of Brazil agreed: "Leadership is critical – the CEO has to be interested in online if it's going to gain traction in the organization." And if that is not convincing enough, let's note the input of Richard Pennycook, CEO of the Co-op Group, who said, "leadership is critical and needs to embrace change, which brings new consumer trends and behaviors into the boardroom and makes sure that management is digitally educated."

    ii. "Leadership needs to be more fungible, excitable, restless in the digital world," said Sebastian James, the Group Chief Executive of Dixons Carphone.

    iii. "Leaders set the strategy and influence the plans – there is no excuse therefore for lack of innovation. It comes from the top," said the CEO of a major UK retail group.

    iv. "Despite being in the business for 14 years, I make an appointment to personally spend 15 to 30 minutes with every candidate before we make them an offer," said Nevzat Aydın, CEO of Yemeksepeti.

    v. "Even when I am on holiday, every customer who sends in a complaint gets a hand-signed letter from me," said John Roberts, the CEO of AO.com.

Andy Street, MD of The John Lewis Partnership, agreed that the governance model is critical: "You need to make sure you have the right Board, a set of managers with the right skills, advisors with objectivity and an [updated] organization which allows you to incorporate new perspectives in an integrated fashion – we now have these" … Which brings us neatly to the tenth principle.

Build a Fit-for-Purpose Organization

It has been found time and time again by hybrid companies that just dropping a group of digitally competent individuals into the middle of the traditional organization will not work.

just dropping a group of digitally competent individuals into the middle of the traditional organization will not work

"Tissue rejection" – which often occurs relatively quickly and brutally – usually smothers and discourages even the most motivated group of digitally oriented individuals. In order to get the best out of such individuals, companies need to build an agile culture of experimentation and learning through failure. The organization which is dealing with the digital elements of the business proposition should typically be able to work at speed, allowing decision-making to be rapid and to take place close to where the digital experiments are taking place. Indeed, many of our interviewees stressed the importance of creating the new ways in which the digital organization needs to operate in terms of philosophy and focus.

John Roberts, CEO of AO.com, has found unique ways to scale up his organization. Firstly, he has ensured that a constant pipeline of talent is available:

> Other organizations tend to recruit by role, but we have a team of four who are constantly recruiting not for role, but for talent. They focus on identifying brilliant people with the right culture and this means that when we need, say ten to 12 programmers, we are able to fill these positions in five to six weeks, from the broader talent pool that our team identifies on an ongoing basis. This is a fraction of the time it would take another business. Our Head of People has been with us for nine years and really understands the profile that we seek.

Secondly, AO.com has codified the cultural traits that the company stands for:

> We have created a DNA test of what we stand for – everyone who joins AO.com has been through this test and it enables us to scientifically

assess their profile and fit with our business. This is a unique capability which enables us to hire the best individuals for our business.

This perspective drives you towards some different organizational models, which would have the following attributes:

1. **Organization design**. In order to deliver the pace and creativity required when operating in the digital world, organizations need to be flatter and relatively autonomous to allow the appropriate level of experimentation and fast development of the appropriate business model. This impacts both structure and responsiveness.

   In terms of structure, there are two considerations. The first relates to whether the organization is ready to accept the new world which is mandated by digital. Sometimes it is better to start off with a new team built outside the existing structure to allow it to thrive and "take off". In these circumstances it is possible to integrate digital capabilities in the core of the business – an objective which must ultimately be the case for all successful hybrid businesses.

   Similarly, you need to decide where in your structure you wish your digital capabilities to reside. This was evidenced by Derk Haank, CEO of Springer, a publisher of scientific journals, where historically each journal was run almost as a separate business unit. In the digital world, he notes that, "In a decentralized business you need to centralize digital initiatives in order to avoid duplication and excessive disruption, as everybody goes off in different directions. Uncontrolled and expensive duplication can become life-threatening."

   In terms of responsiveness, as argued earlier in this book, it is important to enable an empirical approach to proposition development, including a more tolerant attitude to failure. A healthy 80/20 approach to decision making seems to be more appropriate to the digital environment than seeking perfection. All of this is inherent in the new world of Stractics. A number of our interviewees agreed:
   i. "Time is valuable and a source of advantage. I hate to delay decisions – people don't often realize the hidden cost of taking longer

to make a decision in the digital world," said Nevzat Aydın, CEO of Yemeksepeti.

ii. "Always take speed above perfection," said another interviewee.

iii. "We would rather act with 80% confidence than wait to get to 95% confidence as we can always reverse our decisions if they do not play out as expected," reported Nevzat Aydın, CEO of Yemeksepeti.

iv. "I try to balance my time between the day-to-day and the future, and most times our operation is sufficiently ahead of itself to enable me to do that. But there are times when the day-to-day and the future morph – if the site falls over, it becomes all about whatever it takes to get the site back up," said Tim Steiner, the CEO of Ocado.

v. "The fail-fast, agile mind-set is becoming increasingly popular," said Professor Annet Aris of INSEAD.

vi. "We continually re-evaluate our strategy and tactics in light of technology developments and customer feedback," reported Tim Steiner, CEO, Ocado.

2. **Supporting processes**. It's all well and good to fill the above roles with digitally inclined people, but the organization will still risk failure if it doesn't deal with the underlying design of how the organization works. This includes making sure that the following processes are "fit for purpose." The implications for some of an organization's core processes can be profound, for instance …

   i. **HR**. It is not clear that classical HR processes would identify the right sort of people to occupy the digital arena. It would be a really forward-thinking HR function that also understood how to motivate, manage, and incentivize the sort of people who will make the digital revolution happen.

   ii. **Supply chain**. Many pure play and hybrid businesses have a digital front-end but a very conventional back office dedicated to fulfilment of consumer and customer demand. But if the supply chain is not flexible enough to respond to the pace at which the front-end can change – and the importance of on-time delivery is a critical element of customer service, then the company can rapidly become competitively disadvantaged, whether they are a pure play or hybrid.

iii. **Technology**. As we have argued above, the management of technology is a cornerstone of a successful digital business. It is therefore critical that the leadership of the company ensures that there is deep understanding of the difference between front-end technologies which tend to iterate/innovate rapidly and back-end systems which develop on longer timescales. You have to create the right structure and environment in which to optimize both. It is the front-end technologies which tend to move the fastest and hence which require the most attention – "It is difficult to predict the pace of technology innovation, so we need to be flexible to adapt our strategy as new innovations gain ground" (Sachin Bansal, CEO, Flipkart).

iv **Finance**. Pace and uncertainty imply flexibility which does not fit well with most traditional budget processes. The finance process (and the finance director) needs to be prepared for ambiguity and change, as Emre Ekmekçi, Head of Business Development at Turkey's Hepsiburada, explains: "There is no set budget for technology development. It is not a cost centre. We invest as long as we see returns. Similarly in marketing, we have a budget but we increase it or decrease it in response to market changes on a daily or weekly basis." On the other hand, one should not confuse uncertainty with the lack of rigor as Richard Pennycook, CEO of the Co-op Group, observed when he said, "although digital does open new, unknown areas of uncertainty, it is not an excuse to pursue an unprofitable revenue. It certainly deserves risk weighting, but not a blank check." Sir Martin Sorrell, CEO, WPP, went further when he said, "Conviction is important, but numbers do not lie. There are many ways of surrounding a business case with sensible estimations – analysts, clients, and insiders in the digital industry can all be a useful source of insight."

3. **Performance measurement and reward**. The data-driven nature of digital means that businesses are now inundated with a proliferation of potential KPIs and metrics – almost everything can be measured,

and is. Yet, CEOs are clear on the pecking order they have established for the metrics that tell them the most about the health of their business. These are rarely ever sales or financial metrics, but primarily consumer and service-oriented measurements. To the frustration of hybrids, the valuation methodologies for pure plays seldom focus on financial/profit/margin metrics.

In terms of appropriate measures for success in the digital world, a number of common themes can be identified:

• Many obsess – rightly – about net promoter scores (NPS) or alternative measures of Customer Satisfaction. They measure it at every stage of the journey and, for large samples of customers, to enable them to act to improve the levels of satisfaction generated.

"Understanding the 'customer journey' is a key source of insight and action – you need people at every stage in the journey to focus on insight, design, and optimization." (Florian Heinemann of Project A).

• Delivery on time is a key measure of how good the operations team is at enabling customer satisfaction – destroy the last mile performance and you destroy the entire customer experience.
• Low-cost customer acquisition, e.g. share of direct traffic, share of customers through referrals. Cost of acquisition is critical to the economics of the business. Get this wrong and the model will never be profitable.
• Growth and market share, which give the company a read on whether they are outpacing the market.

The timely dissemination of KPIs is key – a number of businesses, e.g. AO.com, have a mobile dashboard which gives everyone from the CEO to the head of the warehouse the relevant metrics, which are updated every two to three minutes. In AO.com's case, 200 individuals within the business have their customized version of the report.

But do not accept any old set of metrics.

The smart money goes back to the fundamentals of the winning business model and what the right set of metrics are which will demonstrate whether it is still on track … Or not!

The bottom line is that the creation of the right culture is critical. "Culture is key, and it has to be guided by two key principles: First, it has to be open to encourage collaboration – sharing information, and encouraging people to make connections across the organization, towards a common goal of improving the customer experience and the business. Second, it needs to encourage individuals to make decisions with the organization's broader objectives in mind – I often tell people I want them to make decisions as if they're their boss's boss," remarked Barney Harford, the CEO of Orbitz.

Elsa Pekmez Atan, EVP of Enpara.com, a Turkish direct-only bank, gave her perspective when she said: "In order to succeed, we have created smaller teams and a flatter organization, which allows us to be very customer-focused and make decisions faster than in the core business [of Finansbank]."

This was confirmed by Dr Hillebrand of Otto when talking about building a fit-for-purpose organization.

> The high-speed digital environment has to be incorporated into your company. You have to incorporate it into the organization in order to reduce the number of interfaces, to enable faster decision-making, and to motivate people to behave accordingly. The traditional hierarchy does not work. We used to have one person on top of the other, and the more senior ones tell the others what to do, and so it goes on in the traditional pyramid. This pyramid does not work anymore. Rather we have to focus on enabling networks of people and project teams to come together to resolve issues and identify solutions. In this environment the task is focused more on bringing good people together, relieving them of the burdens of the traditional organization, and setting up the networks that will allow the company to move fast and in a single-minded way.

Emre Ekmekçi of Hepsiburada agreed: "We have embedded technology teams in every business team. The key difference versus a big box retailer is that we need to be a retailer technology development company if we are to succeed. We are experimenting our way through to the model that works best for us."

While these ten principles are fundamental for both pure plays and hybrids, hybrids in particular need to observe them vigorously. Pure plays, by definition, adopt many of them instinctively. The legacy business models, organizations, and speed of operation inherent in the business models of many hybrids means that you cannot rely on all things to come naturally. A little "brute force from the top" may be required. It is never easy but it can be done, as evidenced by Christian Wegner, board member in charge of digital businesses at ProSiebenSat.1, a successful German hybrid competitor:

"The keys to our success were

- an informed, inspired and ambitious leadership, and with them an aligned and informed board;
- a revitalized organization with executives competent in technology, e-commerce and the need to invest;
- a mandate to internationalize the business as rapidly as possible given the fungibility of our products and our propositions."

8

Strategy Processes in the World of Stractics

Given the need to move at a rapid pace in the digital world and the fact that you can refine/experiment with different digital models rapidly and effectively, strategy is much more an osmotic and empirical process than a purely analytical, logical, or linear process. Strategy and tactics are intertwined.

However, there is still room for a number of elements that are redolent of the traditional strategy era and are important for both pure plays and hybrids to address, irrespective of the approach/process they adopt:

- Companies need a vision as to how they fit into the world, answering such questions as "Why there is a space that could be uniquely ours?" and "How can we occupy that space aggressively to begin with and then defensively as the market matures?"
- Conviction is required about where money is to be made, and the business model which will deliver it.
- You need to determine tactically how you will develop your business model and how you will empirically refine and propagate that model.

- In particular, you need to imagine and plan the growth and scaling-up processes, and how you will deal with the people issues (including succession) that inevitably accompany success.
- Value-crystallization options need to be addressed. Some pure play digital businesses are designed to be sold on to a hybrid (or a bigger pure play) and some to exist as independent businesses. Some hybrids don't even think about value-crystallization, given that they are often public companies and their digital businesses tend to be an integral part of their overall business proposition, not to be hived off, sold off, or otherwise monetized independently. You need to decide early on which option reflects your priorities, as this will fundamentally impact how you implement strategy and think about investment, scaling up, and cash-flow generation.

While these elements appear to be immutable forces of gravity in any sensible strategic process, they are also a useful backcloth to (but not determinant of) the New World strategy process.

Let us begin by revisiting the classical strategy process adopted by most conventional businesses over the last 50 years, and then see how it might be adapted or replaced in the digital world.

Below we have created a diagram which represents the classical strategy process that many companies follow (or should follow; Figure 8.1). It is logical, linear, and delivers a comprehensive articulation of where the business is going, why, and with what consequences.

As we look to the digital world, this process begins to lose relevance in that even the inputs are difficult to pull together in an ecosystem which is changing rapidly, often unpredictably, and with difficult-to-forecast outcomes.

FIGURE 8.1 / A conventional strategy process

So how do digital competitors, particularly pure play companies, think about strategy?

As noted before, most of our pure play interviewees highlighted the need for a vision – whether that is of world-domination or more modest goals – as an essential ingredient in the way the digital world operates. There are so many uncertainties about the rate and direction of techno-logy change and the customer take-up thereof that it makes little sense to try to develop a granular picture of what the next two or three years of operation will look like. This visionary perspective is also recognized by some leading fast-moving consumer goods companies, such as Diageo. Anna Manz, Diageo's head of strategy, observed, "the New World needs a lot more 'future back' thinking. Straightforward analysis will not give you the answers as to how consumer journeys will change and what our responses could be. And these responses will be increasingly global as consumer behaviors converge, thanks to global social media."

Marjorie Scardino, NED at Twitter and former CEO at Pearson, agreed: "Most companies have incremental perspectives, calling for small plans and actions based on what they see today. The digital era calls for bigger, more visionary perspectives about what consumers expect or demand."

Even if you did attempt to define the forward path at such a granular level, you would almost certainly be proved wrong, and possibly quite quickly. As we have mentioned previously, digital enables faster and cheaper innovation and experimentation so that you can try things, see what works, and adjust your plans on very short time horizons.

As one of our more astute pure play interviewees said, "I don't even attempt to put together three-year financials, as the only thing that you would know about them is that they would be wrong."

On the other hand, even the most liberal and tolerant investor needs some indication of the financial needs of the business and when/how that business will deliver value to its shareholders. While three-year plan numbers might remain elusive or misleading, a budget for the following year remains a sine qua non.

Probably more importantly, the business needs to define its action program, even if it is difficult to place precise numbers around it. The business needs to identify what it's going to try to achieve over the next 12 months, and the major programs which will deliver results. The budget therefore reflects these action programs, along with a financial envelope which describes both the revenue side of the business, the operating cost side of the business, and the cost of the major programs/investments.

Interestingly, we have not yet used the word strategy. So far we have only talked about vision, action programs, and budget.

The strategy of the business is, however, somewhat more difficult to define, as it is a result of the vision, tempered by the learnings from the rapidly-flexed action programs. As such, it tends to be a rather fluid concept, involving many changes of direction and business model. This is the world of Stractics!

In this context, most companies operating in the digital world reviewed their strategy on a quarterly basis. By evaluating the outcomes of the many action programs and proposition/technology experiments, they review whether their previous strategic direction remains appropriate or whether it requires minor or major surgery.

In this context, strategy is ephemeral, flexible, and results from the empirical.

In this context, strategy is ephemeral, flexible, and results from the empirical

For pure plays, this is "business as usual." For hybrids, the ambiguity that this environment creates can be deeply unsettling for traditional managers, who are much more used to relative certainty, in terms of what the business will be doing but also regarding the expected financial consequences of doing it. Such managers are "doers" who implement what is required of them. In pure plays, managers tend to be "thinker/doers" – a much scarcer skill set.

We should not be surprised therefore that pure plays and the digital parts of hybrids require a particular form of leadership style, not to mention investor tolerance. Any process put in place to formalize what is happening in the digital arena must reflect these ambiguities and uncertainties.

From our point of view, the following four-step process therefore looks more logical than the classical strategy-development process described above.

Step 1: Start with the Vision, and a Bold One at That!

Having an ambitious vision around which the organization can galvanize is a vital ingredient in a world that is evolving fast and unpredictably. Such a vision is a statement of intent that will inspire people and get them excited about being part of the journey. You need their hearts as well as their wallets in the New World. The vision is not about revenue or profit targets; rather it provides a set of guardrails for the business. If people are in doubt about a particular decision, then reference to the vision will guide them as to what the right decision should be.

Amazon's aim to be earth's most customer-centric business or Google's aim to organize the world's information are two good examples. Or glass-door's vision to be the world's largest career community – these are all suitably uplifting and motivating, and yet not unattainable.

However, the vision also needs to pass the endurance test: if you are changing your vision regularly, it is not a good vision.

Step 2: Establish 90-Day Strategic Goals for Every Team in the Organization and Review Them Every 90 Days

A year is a long time in the Internet age, as confirmed by Otto's Rainer Hillebrand:

> In the digital world, time is of the essence. Everything is fast moving, short lived and dynamic – as a result strategy needs to be reviewed much

more frequently than in the old days. You have to fine tune your strategy much more frequently, not least to reflect the higher speed of innovation.

In other words, having set your vision, don't stop there.

Define the 90-day priorities for everyone in the organization. Everything is changing so fast that 90 days is probably the right recalibration point in terms of whether the strategic objectives and goals are correct, are attainable, and are being delivered. If there is any doubt about any of these then the strategic direction probably needs to be adjusted or changed. Digital organizations are very empirically-oriented – they throw out many different types of experiment, and change direction, on the bases of the outcomes of these experiments. Most of these experiments will deliver within a 90-day framework.

While being clear about the baseline expectations for the next 90 days, objectives should remain in line with the vision – namely, ambitious. People work best with stretching targets, and as one West Coast CEO agreed, "It is better to fall short of a visionary target than exceed a rather conservative one – and it's more fun!" And "Shoot for the moon, because even if you miss, you'll land in the stars."

In setting these 90-day goals/objectives, attention needs to be paid to making sure that all functions in the business are aligned. What you do not want to do is create dysfunctional behavior by having inconsistent objectives. To achieve this alignment, get all the right people in a room and debate the goals, the objectives, and whether they need to be adjusted to reflect organizational stress. This reflects the fact that operating in a digital world requires a far greater degree of cross-functional working than in a traditional enterprise. Commercial teams cannot get anything done without the technology team, the supply chain, and the infrastructure teams all pointing in the same direction.

As Matt Brittin, VP of Google Northern and Central Europe, observed, "You need a quarterly rhythm so that you can reset objectives for everyone, change priorities, and most importantly agree what you are going to stop doing!" Robert Hohman of glassdoor agrees: "When you are moving fast you need to ensure alignment regularly, which involves, in our case, quarterly 'all hands' meetings to share plans, values, and remind people of our overall mission."

One CEO we spoke to takes her entire leadership team away for three days every six months so they can get this cross-functional alignment and a shared set of values in place:

> We have spent a massive amount of time and energy over the last few years taking the entire organization on the journey. The 80 people who lead the organization go through an intense three-day offsite twice a year and we spend time talking about the journey, and they come up with the values which we take great pride in. Ultimately, the top-down direction and the bottom-up actions have to match-up.

Another CEO gets his management team together for half a day every month, in which everyone lines up their priorities on a wall and they go from there – making sure they are all working towards the same outcomes, that everyone is aware of what the others are focused on, and that they close any gaps that exist. If you get this process right then you create huge synergies between "managing the day-to-day" and "building for the long-term;" a good definition of Stractics. "In our organization you have to be able to do both. We hire individuals who can think micro and macro," said Value Retail PLC Group CEO, Desirée Bollier.

Ilker Baydar, CEO of Markafoni, summarizes this well:

> With the impact of the technology over the business strategy, companies, especially in the ecommerce sector, are no longer able to engage in long-term and detailed planning, as it's not realistic, even for two to three years. Obviously we decide on which direction to go in the long run, but we also need to fine-tune our plans in line with the rapid changes emerging from the new technologies and their influence on the public. Our approach to planning is to watch closely the developments in technology, as well as for consumers, and make

quarterly detailed plans. We consider urgency, impact, and importance when making the final decision on what matters most for the organization. So the question is: "What would be stupid for us not to do in the next 90 days?"

Step 3: Refresh and Recalibrate Your Financial Plans Annually

All digital businesses need a three-year financial plan to satisfy banks and/or investors that their money is being put to good use and that there is a profitable future out there somewhere. In addition, these plans support major infrastructure decisions, such as investing in a new warehouse or building a new head office (God forbid).

Such plans, however, are only a broad indication of what the future may hold, given that three years is not a valid planning horizon in a world that is moving rapidly. One West-Coast CEO whose company already had a turnover in the hundreds of millions of dollars indicated that the only thing he could tell you about any numbers he generated beyond year one is that they were wrong. 100% wrong.

Given that many things can change within 12 months, three-year plans can only be a broad indication of what might be financially possible. In this context, companies have to be brutally honest about what they are planning to deliver and the financial and operational consequences thereof.

You also have to be brutally honest a year later about what worked, what did not work, and what, in the context of everything that has been learnt in the last twelve months, you now have to change in terms of your investment strategy over the next three years. Investors in digital businesses understand the uncertainties, and as long as you're open and thoughtful about the implications of change, they will stay with you.

What no investor can stand is lack of transparency and being constantly surprised by adverse impacts. The world is changing fast and it is easy for management teams to say everything is in hand and in control, but everybody knows this is unrealistic. Robert Hohman of glassdoor explained how this works:

> We have to produce numbers, but given the uncertainty of the environment in which we work, they tend to be more aspirational than factual. But our investors are smart and risk-tolerant. You need to explain the total addressable market which will provide the inspiration that underpins value-creation. These investors know that the future is binary – it'll either work big or not at all.

As any experienced executive will tell you, any planning process will be improved by seeking out, from time to time, the harshest critics of the business, be they complaining customers, top suppliers, exiting colleagues, or industry experts so that the business can hear first-hand what they have to say and how the business might be improved. Not all of what they will say be entirely valid, but we are confident that you will learn a few things which will be invaluable and allow you to plan the future with greater insight and understanding.

Desirée Bollier, CEO of Value Retail PLC Group, uses external insight:

> Every time one sees a different model of economy, it is worth thinking of how you might capitalize on this shift. For instance, if you are in the automotive industry, you have to think about what the shared economy and the rise of models like Zipcar means for your business and how you can capitalize on it. Keeping an eye on the shifting sands is imperative in luxury; we will have to face a new generation which is very ethos-oriented, driven to save the planet, and experiencing a polarized society and a backlash from brands. Luxury players will need to win consumers' hearts through a values-based approach that is authentic.

Step 4: Install New Measures of Success

Any goal-oriented organization operating against even 90-day plans needs to be measured and monitored. In the digital world, however, this is very complicated given that in the data-driven nature of digital businesses, there are a myriad of possible KPIs and metrics – almost everything can be measured, and is.

Yet, CEOs need to adopt metrics that really tell them about the health of their business. A number of common themes which emerge from our interviews concern themselves with marketing and sales functions. Such measures are rarely about simply sales or financial metrics. More often they relate to service- and customer-oriented metrics. For instance: all the businesses we spoke to obsessed about Net Promoter Scores, or alternative measures of customer satisfaction. They had the ability to measure this at every stage of the journey for a large sample of customers, which enabled them to diagnose and act to improve the levels of satisfaction that their customers are experiencing.

The measures also need to reflect a comprehensive understanding of the "customer journey." Done correctly this allows the business to create a unique source of insight about customer behavior, which in turn will allow you to redesign and optimize the customer experience.

Another important measure of how effective the business is relates to its cost of customer acquisition. This is driven by the relative share of traffic that comes through referrals, click-throughs, acquisition of databases, etc. Customer acquisition costs can make or break a digital business.

Not only do the marketing and sales people need metrics, but the operations team need to be monitored in terms of such things as accurate measures of delivery on time. Achieving the goal, and/or beating it, is a key measure of how good the operations team is at delivering customer satisfaction – if you fail to deliver a good last mile experience, you destroy the entire customer experience.

Finally, CEOs need to worry about growth and market share. They must therefore focus on measures that give them a read on whether they are outgrowing the market and taking share from competitors not just online but also offline. Within this context, the growth rate in mobile is increasingly a measure that ensures that teams are sufficiently focused on this growing channel!

The dissemination of KPIs on a real-time basis is also key in the fast-moving digital world, as we mentioned on page 103, when we described how AO.com has installed instant access dashboards for many managers.

Following the above four steps will probably deliver most of what you need in terms of guiding your organization, allowing your board to understand your plans and monitor them accordingly, and keeping your shareholders suitably informed about direction and progress.

Nevertheless there are some more operational issues that must form an important part of the planning process. Primarily they focus on people and technology.

In terms of people, the visioning and strategy process has to deliver some very important attributes. The process must deliver:

1. **A clear sense of purpose at the heart of the culture**. There is no doubt that bonuses and stock options do entice employees. On the other hand, most CEOs confirm that it is equally important to make sure that people feel they are at the heart of the strategy of the company, and that they are creating something extraordinary and important. CEOs therefore have to create this sense of purpose in the organization, which will serve to motivate their employees and align their behaviors with the overall strategy and plans of the firm.
2. **An unrelenting focus on talent**. Excellent strategy implemented by less than excellent people just does not work. The DNA of the business must dictate that there is a constant search for outstanding talent and that second best will just not do. It must also cycle underperformers out of the business, to ensure that the average quality of the team is going up over time, not down.
3. **An inspiring and inspired leadership**. Gavin Patterson, CEO of BT, summarized it well when he said, "Companies need to attract and inspire new technologists who are driven not by money and who are only likely to be with you for a while. You require the right sort of leadership to motivate such individuals – leaders who 'get it'."

In terms of technology, it would appear that you need to reconfigure your technology teams frequently and be dynamic in how you prioritize their output. In the technology-intensive digital world, every goal that you set in the process that we have recommended above will have some reliance on the technology development teams. They must therefore not operate in a silo.

It is also true that the technology agenda is usually very long and massively exceeds the available resources. Prioritization and focus are therefore critical. This probably favors the pure plays, who tend to see themselves as technology businesses above everything else. Ocado, Uber, Amazon, and Google spend huge amounts of money on technology versus some of their hybrid competitors.

In summary, we have proposed that businesses in the fast-moving, technology-intense, customer-obsessed digital world should:

- set a vision,
- lay out 90-day plans,
- have annual financial plans,
- design finely-tuned metrics,

all of which are focused on recognizing the fundamental dichotomy of Stractics.

Strategy is no longer a linear process …

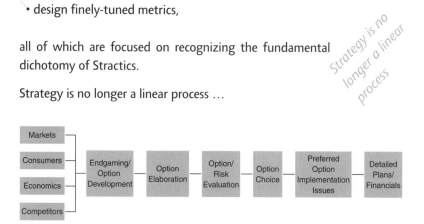

… but has now become an interactive process, operating in the context of a vision and within the constraints of financial parameters.

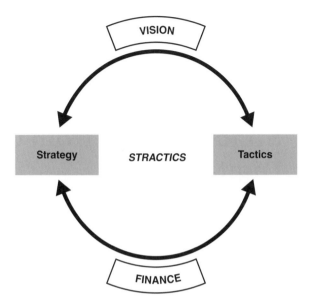

FIGURE 8.2 / Stractics: a non-linear process

9

Advice from the Top: Stractical Tips from Our Digital CEOs

The world looks very different if you are the CEO of a pure play versus being the CEO of a hybrid.

Pure plays find it rather easier to adapt to the world of Stractics than their hybrid competitors. Their going-in hypotheses tend to be simple, visionary, and very long-term. Initially, they do not over-specify the operational environment which will allow them to achieve their vision. Rather they create an iterative/empirical model, which allows them to develop their strategy on the go. As a result, they have to make fewer trade-offs given that there is no existing business competing for funds. In addition, investors tend to be much more tolerant and patient in terms of how the business will ultimately develop and the model that will deliver it. Partly as a result of this, their valuations tend to be more inspirational, allowing funds to be readily available. They are also inherently attractive to the young, geeky, non-financially oriented talent that is so essential to success in the digital world.

Little wonder therefore that the Top Stractics Tips for pure plays are very different from those of hybrids. Even though they live in a seemingly simpler world, that does not necessarily mean that they have it all their own way, or indeed that their business model will succeed. We dealt with this issue in an earlier chapter.

Top Stractics Tips for pure plays are very different from those of hybrids

For those who do have a viable business model, here are the Top Stractics Tips for pure plays from the CEOs we interviewed:

- Get vision/ambition early and only then worry about talent, structure, and finance/risk;
- In terms of the product and proposition, iterate fast and frequently and use the feedback to refine and develop your proposition;
- Focus on market share (of the correctly defined market!), not just revenue growth;
- Think about the monetization options early, as this will inspire funders;
- Build the culture to be talent-friendly – informal, flexible, agile, open, stimulating, rewarding, and easier to engage with;
- Make sure that you invest appropriately in technology (not only IT) and build world-class competence in this competitively differentiating arena;
- Go straight to mobile – it will rule the world. Jim Lawrence, former Chairman of Rothschild North America and a non-executive director at IAG, owner of British Airways, stated: "Mobile is now at the center of e-commerce. For instance, one of the major contributors to the valuation of Alibaba was the strength of its mobile sales;"
- Recognize the need to change leadership at the right inflection point – different skills are required to scale up a company versus creating it.

Sadly, hybrids have a much more complicated time, as they wrestle with a number of rather different but no less critical issues.

hybrids have a much more complicated time

In particular, they are preoccupied (often appropriately) with concerns that entering the world of Stractics will undermine the existing sources of value creation in the current business model. Combine this with the need to simultaneously invest in the new digital world, and the short-term profit impact could be life threatening for the digitally ambitious CEO. Little wonder therefore that the appetite for rapid entry into e-commerce can often be worryingly small in the hybrid corporate landscape.

In addition, few hybrids can honestly say that they are good at creating the right organizational structure and cultural environment to house the rather different type of human capital which is required to be successful in the world of Stractics. This is a particular problem, given the fact that the digital resources are often subject to "tissue rejection" by conventional organizations and traditional managers. This effect is massively magnified by the fact that entirely different incentive schemes and work environments need to be created if you are going to motivate and reward the new digital talent that you require. Sadly, traditional/conventional management often acts as though its nose has been put out of joint when it views the rewards and cultural environment required to attract and retain digital talent.

Brian Newman, head of digital at PepsiCo, has recognized this problem and had a slightly different solution compared with smaller hybrids:

> At a company like ours with 250,000 employees, the challenge is how to introduce new DNA. Just bringing in new sparky, young techies is not a solution. You need to find people already inside your business who have an interest in the digital era and who understand the full speed, flat hierarchies and the openness/permission to fail. If you don't you risk tissue rejection and failure of your digital initiatives.

Nevertheless Brian accepted the need for innovative organizational structures: "even these programs need to be centrally funded and you need to set up separate skunkworks in order for these initiatives to succeed."

If you then compound this series of organizational issues with the fact that new digital business models often have little in common with the conventional business model (at least initially), then CEOs of hybrids truly have huge managerial issues. Putting a digitally-oriented organization alongside a traditional/conventional organization requires considerable leadership skills which will reflect the massive differences between the digital and conventional models in terms of:

- pace, agility and flexibility;
- attitudes to uncertainty and risk;

- an entirely different competitive framework … and series of technology platforms;
- digitally-oriented ways of working, and the work environment.

It is little wonder therefore that perhaps the most important criteria for success in the digital world is for hybrid corporations to have a leadership which gets it and therefore can make all of the difficult trade-offs and investments implied above in the knowledge that the future is definitely as important as, if not more important than, the present or the past.

As a result, the Top Tips for hybrids in the world of Stractics are fundamentally, but not completely, different from those applicable to pure plays.

They are:

- Make sure you have leaders with vision about the role of digital – otherwise the initiative will fall at the first fence;
- Celebrate "cannibalization" and make it a virtue not a crime;
- "Do, not dabble – get stuck in as early movers have advantages and late movers pay a premium," as noted by Anne Tse of Pepsi's China business;
- "Think about your organization structure early and invest in aligning leadership all the way from the board down to management," recommended Christian Wegner, board member of ProSiebenSat.1.

At the beginning, build your digital capability in a separate unit, to protect it from the overwhelming administrative and cultural burden of the conventional business; if you don't, Stractics will be smothered at birth. Create a fully integrated, multichannel, consumer-oriented business model consistent with the world of Stractics as a later, but critical, step.

- At the point of integration, ensure that performance KPIs and incentives are aligned, so that both conventional and digital initiatives are motivated to optimize the overall value creation for the business, e.g. the way that The John Lewis Partnership incentivizes store managers to use digital in the store.

- Do not rush to put your IT director in charge of technology. You will need to build a consumer technology (CT) capability in parallel with your existing IT platform development to create competitive advantage.
- Empower the geeks by building an appropriate culture, motivation, and reward-environment – and make sure that the rest of the organization understands why these people are "different." "Create a new open culture where the whole team can provide opinions on any technology, customer, or channel issues," advised Elsa Atan, EVP of Enpara.com in Turkey.
- Educate the rest of the business about the threats and opportunities created by the digital world and the need to respond to them in a single-minded and bold way.

Operationally, the important things to do are:

- commit 110% to a focused (and possibly quite small) series of digital goals/objectives in order to get a toe in the water and allow the digital model to engage with the conventional model;
- standardize as much as possible as early as possible so as to limit degrees of uncertainty and unconstructive debate;
- tolerate uncertainty, ambiguity, and failure and incorporate it into "business as usual" – the digital world requires rapid and frequent iteration, as strategy is often developed empirically;
- create "burning platforms," so that the organization moves with pace (even urgency), flexibility, and agility.

Both pure plays and hybrids have huge challenges to operate and succeed in the new digital world where pace, urgency, technology, and changing consumer behavior all militate in favor of new types of leadership, organization, cultures, and strategies.

This is the new world, in which Stractics is the name of the game.

chapter 10

The Future of Stractics

Throughout this book we have used the titles **pure play** and **hybrids** in order to emphasize the two extremes of players in the digital world. Pure plays have no legacy assets, while hybrids start off with no digital assets.

The real world is never quite that simple, of course.

As we have described in the previous chapters, many pure plays have very conventional back offices, even though their consumer interface might very well be digital. Equally, successful hybrids treat digital both as one of the many routes to market, and as a way of communicating with consumers, thus complementing their traditional business models.

In the long term, however, we can already observe that these extremes will not reflect the reality of many markets. As we tried to demonstrate in Chapter 6, it is overly simplistic in many sectors to think that either pure plays or hybrids will "win." We already observe that Amazon is opening its first store in New York and Zappos is opening its first store in Las Vegas.

This blurring of distinctions around the extremes will likely continue, and we will get increasingly comfortable with digital being part of "Business As Usual." Indeed many interviewees – particularly from hybrids – indicated that market reaction to the fast pace of digital developments was slightly panicky, and that digital is now being integrated into day-to-day business processes in many companies and industries.

The CEO of *The Times* of London, Mike Darcey, commented,

> In the early days of digital, all retailers were told that they were doomed. Indeed Argos was told by all the analysts to "sell all its stores." Nowadays nobody would propose such a drastic solution. Indeed Amazon is investing in "click and collect" pickup points, which is precisely the business model which Argos represents. Similarly, newspapers initially overreacted by giving away their hard earned content for free. Nowadays it is been proven that you can charge consumers for quality digital information as well as the print product. In this sense, forward-looking hybrids have already become digital companies. We will recognize this fully when we hybrids stop using the word "digital."

Antoine de Saint-Affrique, former President of Foods at Unilever, concurred when he said that

> digital is just part of the environment and business as usual. You need to understand the ecosystem in which you're operating, and nowadays digital is part of that. It provides massively enhanced forms of engagement with your consumers, to whom you can provide more information on things like provenance and the product itself. We can also describe how we work with farmers and we can identify how consumers can participate and interact with our brands. As such, success in the digital world comes from strategic clarity. You need to understand what is happening to your ecosystem, and then how you will make it work to your advantage. In this context, data is critical and you need people in-house who thoroughly understand what you can get out of it.
>
> "In summary, you need to be able to transform at the rate that the market transforms. You need to think about what's happening not just 'process it'."

Jim Lawrence, former Chairman of Rothschild North America and non-executive director of IAG, owner of British Airways and Iberia agreed: "Any successful business breeds contempt for change. But nowadays markets and technology change very rapidly. If you have not got digital as part of your general strategy, it is flawed."

And there are great examples of how both pure plays and hybrids have successfully taken advantage of the huge opportunities created by the increasing digitization of many markets. Lego is amongst them. Jørgen Vig Knudstorp, Lego's CEO, emphasized this when he observed: "Our company has benefited hugely from the digital era, where we have been able to enjoy the benefits of massive Internet communities on Facebook, etc. Indeed Lego is the second most watched brand on YouTube despite the fact that we have only produced less than 1% of the Lego content. Our consumers and customers are our best digital marketeers."

It is probably not necessary to describe here the many well-known pure play successes. We are all using them constantly – Google, Facebook, Instagram, etc.

Hybrid successes, however, are sometimes less obvious, and hence we thought we would finish our book by recounting the story of Business Monitor International, who successfully and very profitably transformed their business at the very time at which other print media businesses were failing to respond to the "Stractical" world. Business Monitor International published macroeconomic/financial research in hard copy form to a relatively small set of corporate customers.

The founders of BMI Research, Richard Londesborough and Jonathan Feroze, must be congratulated on navigating extremely choppy waters so well. Their story should be an inspiration to all hybrids and is a great call to act early and reinvent yourselves appropriately.

Richard and Jonathan's story is as follows:

> Going digital unlocked huge value for us. Originally our business was focused on print subscriptions and often in emerging markets. With the dot-com boom it was clear we needed to innovate if we were going to

protect our markets. Initially we grafted a digital product on top of our print product. Nevertheless it became clear quite quickly that content was going to need to transform, given that even internal IT was going digital, not to mention our interface with the customer, and the customers' access to the product. This meant that things like daily rather than monthly updates to our market reports were going to have to be instituted. They were not a "nice to have" feature, but "critical to have."

As we adopted digital we found that we could diversify not only in terms of the relevance of our existing products, but we could also launch new products in new sectors and in new countries relatively easily. In addition the Internet made it easier for our customers to upgrade both in terms of the number of products that they purchased but also the number of seats that were included in the package. More explanation of the product was required and customer expectations of our service went up dramatically. Finally, digitization allowed our product to be inserted into the workflow of our customers which was massively enhanced by the fact that analysis of our database by customers became possible, not to mention the fact that visualization of the products allowed better comprehension of our reports and how they could be used.

Our product portfolio therefore became more valuable, but also much more complex in terms of selling it to customers, and this complexity required a face-to-face sales force in order to explain the product suite to sophisticated corporate purchasers.

We invested significantly, therefore, in building an international sales force and were rewarded by a massive increase in the average "ticket price" of each customer – it went up ten-fold – at a time when our subscriber base fell by almost 50%, our revenues quintupled.

We originally thought that the digital world would undermine our business model and that of our competitors. In some senses it did, given that the old business model fell over and ceased to be relevant. On the other hand, digital created huge opportunities, which we were able to grasp and which massively increased the value of our business.

The business is neither pure play nor hybrid. It is now a fully integrated business using digital and physical attributes to optimize its value and strategy.

For pure plays and hybrids alike, therefore, the messages are clear.

- Be obsessed by your customers and their "journey."
- Keep on top of technology and the way in which it is progressively changing consumer behavior.
- Rethink your organization, culture, and talent acquisition strategies in order to make sure that you can access and retain the skills which will allow you to be successful in the digital world.
- Ensure that the leadership of the company buys into the new world and is therefore open to grasping opportunities, and do not only think of "digital" as a threat or a problem.

By following these simple concepts, pure plays and hybrids will increasingly converge and "digital" as a word will cease to be a useful way of describing the old or the new world.

As a consequence, Stractics will be fully integrated into the core business model.

Strategic insight will simultaneously be developed empirically as well as as a result of longer-term strategic thinking. It will not be either pure plays or hybrids who win. Rather it will be those companies who are able to integrate conventional thinking with new world thinking, to create sustainable competitive advantage and the value that goes with it.

pure plays and hybrids will increasingly converge

As a consequence, Stractics will be fully integrated into the core business model.

Acknowledgements

I have already paid tribute to the ever vigilant and constructive input of my partner, Anita Balchandani. I do have to add others who have also made this book possible. Foremost amongst them must be my assistant, Jo Falcon-Cross, whose endless patience is one of the wonders of the world. Fiona O'Sullivan also provided invaluable support.

My fellow OC&C Strategy Consultants partners must also be thanked for helping to identify and set up all the interviews. Of course the input of the interviewees has been priceless in terms of adding insight and perspective to such a complex topic. In addition, a couple of my partners have provided invaluable challenges in terms of critiquing early versions of this manuscript.

Finally, the analysis which resulted in the graphics contained in the book was the result of a lot of hard work by Caroline Heap, Alexia Rousselin, Guy Ward Thomas, and Stephen Carolin. Jocelyn Corner helped create important parts of the text.

A lot of work goes into creating a book, and it is never the work of one individual; this is no exception. The efforts of all us consultants were admirably pulled together by John Bond and Silvia Crompton, who have masterminded the editing and creation of this book.

To all of these collaborators, thank you.

Chris Outram

Contributor Biographies

Keith Allen – Mecom

Keith Allen joined Mecom in 2004, was appointed Group Finance Director in 2006, and became Chief Operating Officer in 2008. A chartered accountant, he joined the Corporate Finance division of Hambros Bank Limited in 1989, becoming a Director and Head of the media team in 1997. In 1998, he left Hambros to become joint head of the newly established Corporate Finance division at BNP, and following BNP's acquisition of Paribas in 2000, he assumed responsibility for the UK media team. Additionally, he is a governor of Alderbrook Primary School.

Annet Aris – INSEAD

Annet Aris has been adjunct Professor of Strategy at INSEAD since 2003, where she developed and teaches the MBA course "Media, Internet and the Digital Transition." She was nominated two years running for best teacher by MBA students. She is a board member of the Sanoma Group, a European TV broadcaster and educational publisher, and of the Kabel Deutschland AG (Munich) and TV broadcaster ProSiebenSat.1. She is also a board member for several non-media companies. Annet is a Dutch native and received a MSc from the University of Wageningen and has an MBA from INSEAD, after which she worked for McKinsey & Company in the Netherlands, the UK and Germany, becoming a partner. She has written many articles and is a weekly columnist in the Dutch *Financial Times* (*Financieel Dagblad*).

Nevzat Aydın – Yemeksepeti

Nevzat Aydın is Co-Founder and global CEO of Yemeksepeti, the leading online food-delivery portal in Turkey. Yemeksepeti has recently expanded into the Middle East with the global brand Foodonclick.com, which currently serves the UAE, Oman, Qatar, Saudi Arabia, Lebanon, and Greece. In 2010, Nevzat Aydın was chosen as the "Most Successful Young Entrepreneur in Turkey" by *CNBC Business* magazine. Mr Aydın was among 150 entrepreneurs from all around the world invited to attend the Entrepreneurship Summit held by US President Barack Obama in April 2010. Mr Aydın has received the Lenovo Doer Award as the "Most Inspiring Entrepreneur" and was named first on Fortune's "40 Under 40" list in 2013.

Eduardo Baek – eÓtica

Mr Baek started his career as a management consultant at Value Partners in 2000. In 2002, he pursued opportunities as an entrepreneur in education and construction materials. After receiving his MBA from Stanford, Mr Baek founded eÓtica, a specialized e-tailer focused on eyewear.

Sachin Bansal – Flipkart

Sachin Bansal is Co-Founder and CEO of Flipkart, India's leading e-commerce marketplace. Sachin oversees the company's strategic development, overall direction and business management. Sachin has pioneered innovations that have redefined the e-commerce ecosystem in India. An Indian software engineer and Internet entrepreneur, Sachin graduated from IIT-Delhi with a degree in Computer Engineering. An avid gaming enthusiast, Sachin likes to spend most of his free time with his family.

Ilker Baydar – Markafoni

Ilker Baydar has been CEO of Markafoni Group of Companies, a subsidiary of Naspers Group, since his appointment in May 2014. Ilker, a graduate of political sciences at Marmara University, completed his e-MBA degree in Sabancı University and participated in the Leadership Development Program at Harvard Business School. He commenced his career in 1997 in Group Promodes Continent as Category Manager. He worked as Group

Manager in Turkey and Group Director in China for Metro Cash & Carry until 2008, then as Commercial Director for Best Buy and Darty in Turkey between 2008 and 2012. He was General Manager of Hepsiburada.com until he joined the Markafoni Group.

Jan Bayer – BILD and WELT Group

Jan Bayer was appointed President of the BILD and WELT Group in 2014, following a career in media. He began his career as a trainee at the *Süddeutsche Zeitung* in Munich and worked there from 1996 to 1999 in advertising sales. Following a stint as Publishing Manager of the *Volksstimme* in Magdeburg, he returned to the *Süddeutsche Zeitung* in 2002 as Head of Controlling, becoming Publishing Manager in 2004. Then he became the Head of the Executive Office for Newspapers at Axel Springer SE, and then Publishing Director of the Hamburg Regional Newspaper Group, and Chairman of the management board of the WELT Group/Berliner Morgen-Post/Hamburger Abendblatt from 2008.

Desirée Bollier – Value Retail Plc

Desirée Bollier graduated with a degree in Corporate Law and studied Philosophy in Paris. Her career spans 30 years within retail, the last 13 of which have been as Chief Executive of Value Retail, founding and overseeing the management of the Chic Outlet Shopping® Villages in Europe and China. Prior to this, Bollier was with Ralph Lauren for 14 years, culminating as Senior Vice President of Retail for Europe, MEA, and GIC countries. Bollier is a board member of Value Retail and sits on the corporate board of the Royal Academy. She is also a member of the World Travel & Tourism Council (WTTC).

Toon Bouten – Tomorrow Focus AG

Toon Bouten is an internationally experienced manager who has been CEO of several European companies and was appointed Chief Executive of Tomorrow Focus AG in January 2013. Prior to joining Tomorrow Focus AG, Toon was CEO of European Directories, a local search and lead generation specialist based in Amsterdam and London, with operations throughout Europe. Before this he was President and CEO of the Danish headset maker GN Netcom and led the European business of Philips Electronics' Consumer Electronics division. Prior to this he worked at a number of international ICT companies, including serving as Vice President and General Manager at Compaq Computers, where he built up the consumer segment in the Europe, Middle East, and Africa region. After graduating in engineering, Toon Bouten began his career in 1984 with Philips in the Netherlands.

Matt Brittin – Google

Matt Brittin is Vice President, Google Europe, leading business and operations in the UK, Germany, Benelux, the Nordics, and beyond. He serves on the boards of Sainsbury's, and charities The Media Trust and The Climate Group. Previously he worked in the newspaper industry, at McKinsey & Company, and in real estate, having graduated from Cambridge University, where he often came second in the Oxford and Cambridge Boat Race. Matt won World Championship medals rowing for Great Britain, was a member of the 1988 Olympic team, and more recently raised funds for the Paralympics by cycling the length of Britain in the rain.

Mark Britton – Avvo

Mark is the Founder and CEO of Avvo, the world's largest community for legal guidance and services. Prior to founding Avvo, Mark was the Executive Vice President of Worldwide Corporate Affairs of InterActiveCorp Travel (IACT) and Expedia, Inc. In this position, Mark oversaw all accounting, finance, strategy, corporate development, legal, human resources, and government relations functions for the IACT companies, including Expedia, Hotels.com, Hotwire, Classic Custom Vacations, and Interval International. Mark was also Expedia's first general counsel and, today, he sits on the Board of Directors of Orbitz Worldwide. With Avvo's success, Mark regularly speaks on technology, consumer, and legal issues. He received Ernst & Young's "Entrepreneur of the Year" Award in 2015 and was previously named a "Seattle Top 25 Innovator" and "Tech Titan 2.0" by Seattle business magazines. Mark received his law degree from George Washington University. He holds a degree in finance from Gonzaga University and serves on Gonzaga's Board of Regents.

Jerry Buhlmann – Aegis

Jerry has over 30 years' experience in the media and advertising industries. He started his career at Young & Rubicam, before moving to WCRS. In 1989 he founded BBJ, later renamed Vizeum, and built the business before it was acquired by Aegis Media in 1999. In 2003 he was appointed CEO of Aegis Media EMEA and then Chief Executive of Aegis Group Plc in 2010. In 2012 Jerry negotiated the sale of Aegis Group Plc to Dentsu Inc., a £3.2-billion transaction which remains the largest deal in the history of advertising, following which he was appointed CEO of Dentsu Aegis Network. In July 2013 Jerry became only the second non-Japanese Executive Officer of Dentsu Inc.

Brian Cassin – Experian

Brian Cassin is Chief Executive Officer of Experian, having joined it in 2012 as Chief Financial Officer, bringing with him 20 years of experience in the corporate financial advisory sector. Brian was a close and trusted advisor to the Experian Group for over eight years before joining the company. He was a strategic advisor to the board of GUS in 2006, during the establishment of Experian as a publicly listed company. Prior to joining Experian, Brian was Co-Head of the European business of global investment banking firm Greenhill & Co. Having joined Greenhill as one of the founding members in 1998, Brian played a significant role in building the business in Europe and establishing Greenhill as an internationally recognized, market-leading independent corporate advisory firm.

Patrick Cescau – InterContinental Hotels Group Plc

Patrick Cescau is Non-Executive Chairman of InterContinental Hotels Group Plc. From 2005 to 2008, he was Group Chief Executive of Unilever Group, having previously been Chairman of Unilever Plc, Vice-Chairman of Unilever NV, and Foods Director, following a career with the company which began in France in 1973. Prior to being appointed to the Board of Unilever Plc and Unilever NV in 1999, as Finance Director, he was Chairman of a number of the company's major operating companies and divisions, including in the US, Indonesia, and Portugal. He was formerly a Senior Independent Director and Non-Executive Director of Pearson

Plc and a Director at INSEAD. Patrick is also currently a Non-Executive Director of International Consolidated Airlines Group S.A., a trustee of The Leverhulme Trust, and a patron of the St Jude India children's charity.

Mike Darcey – News UK

Mike Darcey took up the position of Chief Executive Officer of News UK in January 2013, following 15 years with BSkyB, where he was Chief Operating Officer from 2006. Mike is credited with focusing the company's strategy to secure a profitable future for News UK and with spearheading the decision to move the London operations into one building with HarperCollins and Dow Jones. He is also a Non-Executive Director and Senior Independent Director of Home Retail Group (which operates Argos and Homebase). Darcey graduated from Victoria University in Wellington with an Honours degree in Mathematics and has an MSc from the London School of Economics. He was a national gymnastics champion in New Zealand as a teenager.

Asmita Dubey – L'Oréal China

Asmita Dubey is the Chief Marketing Officer of L'Oréal China. An Indian, with her initial working years spent in India, Asmita is a marketing professional with 18 years spent in international communication groups and corporates in India, the Middle East, and China, which have enabled her to accumulate a deep understanding of the markets and consumer behavior in India and China. Asmita joined L'Oréal China in January 2013 as Chief Marketing Officer in charge of digital marketing, e-commerce marketing, marketing research, integrated marketing communications, strategic media planning, and corporate consumer advisory services. Prior to L'Oréal, Asmita was at Mindshare (WPP group) for eight years.

Emre Ekmekçi – Hepsiburada

Emre Ekmekçi is President, Business Development, at Dogan Online Group Companies. Founded in 1999, Dogan Online Group consists of the leading e-commerce and betting businesses in Turkey with brands such as Hepsiburada.com, Nesine.com, Evmanya.com and 6cadde.com. He is tasked with building new businesses, new venture identification and continuous improvement to the group companies through value-added business models. Prior to Dogan Online, in partnership with European Founders Fund and Rocket Internet, Emre pioneered the daily deal business in Turkey, by launching Groupon's Turkish operations and its local Turkish brand Sehirfirsati.com, making it a market leader company in less than 18 months. Emre has global experience in Interactive Marketing, having served for eight years at a leading full-service agency in Los Angeles, with a focus on global business development, and has worked in Los Angeles, Chicago, Hong Kong, Shanghai, London, and Paris. Emre has an MBA with honors from Columbia Business School and holds a Bachelor of Science degree in Industrial and Systems Engineering from the University of Southern California. A native of Adana, Emre is also a proud alumnus of Tarsus American High School.

Vitor Falleiros – Dafiti
Mr Falleiros holds the position of Head of Planning and Control for Dafiti, a leading Brazilian e-tailer focused on fashion. Before joining Dafiti, Mr Falleiros worked for the retail bank Itaú, and was a management consultant at Bain, serving clients in diverse industries such as retail, airline, and oil and gas.

Jonathan Feroze – BMI Research
Jonathan Feroze founded and edited the bilingual business newspaper *Encuentro*, published by the *Mexico City News*, following which, in 1984, he co-founded Business Monitor International (now renamed BMI Research), a leading provider of country risk and industry analysis. The company rapidly expanded, serving customers in over 140 countries, and in 1997 was honored with the Queen's Award for Exports. BMI provides specialist business intelligence to over 400 of the Fortune 500; the company is headquartered in London, with offices around the world. BMI was acquired by Fitch Group in 2014, and Jonathan now serves as a Non-Executive Director for Fitch Information Services. He has since set up (with BMI Co-Founder Richard Londesborough) Sevenex Capital Partners, a venture partnership backing early stage businesses across the UK.

Jonathan Gabbai – eBay

As Head of International Mobile Product at eBay, Jonathan is responsible for a broad range of innovation. His most recent focus has been developing the Red Laser app for Windows Mobile and the eBay application for Windows 8. Before moving into mobile product at eBay, Jonathan spent three years in mobile marketing looking after eBay browser extensions. During his time at eBay he has worked with Mozilla, Microsoft, Apple, and Google, as well as many other internationally renowned market leaders in both retail and technology. He holds an Engineering Doctorate in Complex Emergent Systems, a Diploma in Management Sciences, and a degree in Aerospace Engineering.

Krishnan Ganesh – Portea Medical

Ganesh is a successful serial entrepreneur with four successful green-field ventures and exits. His last venture, TutorVista, was acquired by Pearson for $213 million. He was among the top five nominees for the *Economic Times* Entrepreneur of the year 2012 Award and has been recognized as an "Iconic Entrepreneur of India" by the Indian Government. His current venture, Portea Medical, provides technology-led home healthcare to the Indian consumer. He is a promoter of several Indian consumer Internet and e-commerce companies, including Bigbasket.com, India's largest eGrocery company. Previously, Ganesh founded Marketics, which was sold for $63 million in 2007, and he was also CEO of Wipro/Bharti British Telecom – a British Telecom JV in India.

Jean-Christophe Garbino – Kiabi

Garbino has, since 2007, been CEO of Kiabi, a $2 billion French omni-channel retail fashion company operating 450 stores in eight countries. Before taking on the role of CEO of Kiabi, Garbino was general manager of Kiabi, Spain, and prior to this was an account manager at AXA UAP. His vision of leadership is to free and empower every employee to have them lead the business.

Marc van Gelder – Peapod and Mediq

Marc van Gelder is the former CEO of Mediq and currently a Supervisory Board Member of several companies, such as Maxeda, Action, and Gimv.

In addition he is a trustee of several charitable organizations, such as the Helen Dowling Institute and the Royal Palace "Het Loo."

Derk Haank – Springer Science + Business Media

Derk Haank was appointed CEO of Springer Science+Business Media in February 2004. After obtaining a degree in Economics and Business Administration and spending some years as a researcher at the Vrije Universiteit Amsterdam, Mr Haank began his career in publishing in 1986 at Elsevier Science, where he held various management positions, spending part of this time based in the UK. He was appointed CEO of Misset, Elsevier's B-to-B division, in 1991. From 1998 to 2004, Mr Haank was CEO of Elsevier Science and was also an Executive Board member at Reed Elsevier. In the little spare time he has, he is a passionate reader and loves sports.

Rick Hamada – Avnet

Rick Hamada became CEO of Avnet Inc. in 2011, having joined Hamilton/ Avnet Electronics in 1983 as a Technical Specialist. His career evolved to encompass sales and leadership roles with the company, including Field Sales Representative, Regional Sales Manager, and Vice President of Business Development. Mr Hamada was named in *Computer Reseller News*'s "Top 25 Most Influential Channel Executives" three times. He served as Chairman of the Global Technology Distribution Council, an industry consortium representing the world's leading IT distributors. He currently serves on the board of directors of Keysight Technologies, a global electronic measurement technology and market leader. Mr Hamada holds a Bachelor of Science degree in Finance from San Diego State University, where in 2009 he was named as a member of the advisory board of its College of Business Administration.

Michael E. Hansen – Cengage Learning

Michael E. Hansen became CEO of Cengage Learning in 2012, having previously served as CEO of Elsevier Health Sciences, a division of Reed Elsevier. Prior to this he was President and CEO of Harcourt Assessment, which was then the education arm of Reed Elsevier. Earlier, Mr Hansen was Executive Vice President at Bertelsmann, a $20-billion global media company, and prior to this he held various posts with the Boston Consulting Group in New York, ultimately becoming Partner and Co-Chairman of the e-Business and Media Practice. Mr Hansen is currently a Board Member of the American Institute for Contemporary German Studies. He holds a Master of Law degree from the University of Bonn in Germany and an MBA from Columbia University in New York.

Barney Harford – Orbitz Worldwide

Barney Harford has served since 2009 as CEO and Director of Orbitz Worldwide, a global online travel company operating brands including Orbitz.com, CheapTickets, ebookers, and HotelClub in the United States, Europe, and the Asia Pacific region. Barney previously served in a variety of roles at Expedia, Inc. from 1999 to 2006, including as President of Expedia Asia Pacific from 2004 to 2006, leading the company's entry into China, Japan, and Australia. Prior to Expedia, Barney worked in the UK as a strategy consultant with The Kalchas Group. Barney is a member of the US Department of Commerce's Travel and Tourism Advisory Board, the US Travel Association's CEO Roundtable, and serves as Board member of LiquidPlanner, having previously served on the Board of eLong, Orange Hotel Group, and GlobalEnglish.

Florian Heinemann – Project A

Florian Heinemann is Co-Founder and Managing Director of Project A Ventures. Previously, he was Managing Director of Rocket Internet, and was Co-Founder and Managing Director of JustBooks/AbeBooks, which was sold to Amazon in 2002. Additionally he co-led the online marketing department of Jamba! and the online dating portal iLove (2003–05, exit to Verisign). He has been an investor/business angel in more than 40 startups, e.g. AdScale, Ladenzeile, Netmoms, and Tradoria. Florian holds a Doctorate in Innovation Management/Entrepreneurship from RWTH Aachen University, and a Masters degree in Business Administration from WHU Koblenz.

Rainer Hillebrand – Otto Group

Dr Hillebrand was appointed Vice CEO of Otto Group in 2007. Otto Group is a worldwide operating retail contractor active in over 20 countries.

Dr Hillebrand has been a member of the company's executive board since 1999. He joined the company as the Head of Strategy Development in 1990. Prior to that, he was an independent consultant. He holds a Doctoral degree from the University of the German Federal Armed Forces, which he entered after having become an officer.

Robert Hohman – Glassdoor

Robert Hohman is Co-Founder and CEO of Glassdoor, a leading jobs and recruitment community. Before creating Glassdoor, Robert was most recently President of Hotwire, a leading discount travel site and division of Expedia, Inc. He was also one of the original team members of Expedia, and was part of the executive team that took it public in 1999. Robert started his career at Microsoft and worked as a software developer in a range of areas from Windows 95 to interactive television to online games. Robert serves on the US Economic Development Administration's National Advisory Council on Innovation and Entrepreneurship (NACIE). He holds Bachelors and Masters degrees in Computer Science from Stanford University.

Jeffrey R. Holzschuh – Morgan Stanley

Jeffrey Holzschuh is Chairman of Morgan Stanley's Institutional Securities Group, Chairman of its Global Power and Utility Group, and a member of the firm's Management Committee. Jeffrey joined Morgan Stanley in 1983, since when he has worked in its New York and Los Angeles offices and been actively involved in many of the energy industry's largest mergers and acquisitions. He was appointed by the US Secretary of Energy to serve on the US Electricity Advisory Board, served as Chair of the EEI Wall Street Advisory Group and was a founding member of the US Partnership for Renewable Energy Finance (USPREF). He serves on several charitable and academic boards, including as Chairman of the Niagara University Board of Trustees.

Mark Hunter – Molson Coors Brewing Company

A graduate from the University of Strathclyde, Mark has spent the last 32 years in a variety of sales, marketing and general management positions, primarily in Europe and North America. As President and CEO of Molson Coors Brewing Company, based in Denver, Colorado, Mark leads one of the world's leading beer companies, with extraordinary brands such as Coors, Molson, Carling and Staropramen. The Molson Coors purpose is to "Delight the World's Beer Drinkers," and Mark is a passionate believer in championing beer and building respect for the category through responsible drinking.

Sebastian James – Dixons Carphone

Sebastian James was appointed Group Chief Executive of Dixons Carphone in August 2014, following the merger of Dixons Retail Group with Carphone Warehouse. He joined Dixons in April 2008 and held various roles, including Group Operations Director, prior to his appointment as Group Chief Executive in February 2012. Before joining Dixons Retail, Sebastian was CEO of Synergy Insurance Services Limited and gained wide retail experience as Strategy Director responsible for developing and implementing the turnaround strategy at Mothercare. He started his career at The Boston Consulting Group, having completed an MBA at INSEAD and an MA at Oxford University. Sebastian is also a Non-Executive Director of Direct Line Insurance Group Plc and trustee of the charities Save the Children and Tablets for Schools.

Jørgen Vig Knudstorp – LEGO Group

Jørgen Vig Knudstorp is the CEO and President of the LEGO Group, which has more than 14,000 employees in more than 45 countries. The company is one of the world's leading manufacturers of play materials and has an ambition to eventually reach every child in every country with a LEGO® play experience. After three years as a consultant at McKinsey, Knudstorp joined the LEGO Group in 2001 as Director with responsibility for specific strategic development efforts, and quickly progressed to take on top management positions within Strategic Development and Corporate Affairs. He was appointed CEO and President in 2004, with the primary task of securing the LEGO Group's survival in a time of crisis and subsequently preparing the company for growth, and under him the company has undergone a significant financial and commercial revitalization, more than quadrupling its sales. In 2006 he was named Denmark's "Leader of the Year." Knudstorp holds a PhD in Business Economics. His research was done at MIT in Boston, USA, and at Aarhus University in Denmark.

Alexander Kudlich – Rocket Internet
Alexander Kudlich joined Rocket Internet in 2011, where he is Group Managing Director, responsible for operations, product development, technology and resources. In 2005, upon graduation from University College, London, Alexander joined Axel Springer AG as the Assistant of the Chairman and CEO (Dr Mathias Döpfner). From 2008 to 2011, he worked in various managerial positions in a group company of Axel Springer AG – zanox.de AG – including as Regional Managing Director for Asia Pacific and Central and Eastern Europe. He has a degree from the University of St Gallen in Switzerland, an MA in Philosophy from University College, London, and an MBA from the European School of Management and Technology.

James A. Lawrence – Rothschild North America
Jim Lawrence has served as CEO of Rothschild North America, and Co-Head of Global Investment Banking at the firm, where he is currently Chairman. Prior to joining Rothschild, Lawrence was Chief Financial Officer at Unilever and Executive Director on the boards of Unilever NV and Plc. He has also held positions as Executive Vice President of Northwest Airlines and President and CEO of Pepsi-Cola Asia, Middle East, Africa. He was Co-Founder and Chairman of The LEK Partnership, and previously was a Partner of Bain and Company and headed their London and Munich offices. He has served on 15 public company boards since 1990 and is a Non-Executive Director at International Airline Group, the holding company of British Airways and Iberia.

Richard Londesborough – BMI Research
Richard Londesborough is the Co-Founder of Business Monitor International, now known as BMI Research, a leading provider of country risk and industry analysis and data. The company grew from two staff in one small office in 1984, to 300 employees in five continents by 2014, when it was acquired by Fitch Group. Richard now serves as a Non-Executive Director for

Fitch Information Services, and has set up (with BMI Co-Founder Jonathan Feroze) venture partnership Sevenex Capital Partners. Richard graduated from Exeter University, having worked for one year as a sports reporter in Iran. Richard joined the *Mexico City News* after graduating, covering finance and politics, and corresponded for Reuters and *The Sunday Times* before setting up Latin America Monitor in 1984 in London, later to become BMI, which won the Queen's Award for Exports.

Guilherme Loureiro – Walmart

Guilherme Loureiro joined Walmart Brazil in 2012 as Executive Vice-President and became the company's President in September 2013. Prior to joining Walmart, Loureiro worked at Unilever for 24 years, serving in several strategic roles in Brazil and internationally, among them as Chairman of the company's Mexican operations. Loureiro received his Bachelor's degree in Business Administration from Getúlio Vargas Foundation (FGV), the same institution where he earned his Master's and Doctorate degrees. Loureiro is also a graduate of TGPM – The General Manager Programme of Harvard Business School. He is also a member of YPO (Young Presidents' Organization).

Dan Mallin – Magnet 360

As a Board Member, Co-Founder and Managing Partner of Magnet 360, Dan helps companies leverage marketing and technology to provide competitive differentiation and engagement for outcomes. Dan sits on multiple boards, bringing a differentiating viewpoint, helping organizations evaluate opportunities and facilitating governance oversight as an agent of change. He has received multiple 3M awards, Ernst & Young's Entrepreneur of the Year, *Business Journal*'s "40 under 40," Twin Cities Business "200 People to Know," and the Minnesota Business "Real Power 50." Dan has also served as a Chief Officer at multiple companies recognized as "best places to work" in multiple markets nationally.

Paul Manduca – Prudential

Paul has been Chairman of Prudential since 2012, where he previously served as a board member and Senior Independent Director. Prior to this, Paul was a Non-Executive Director of Wm Morrison Supermarkets Plc, where he also chaired the Remuneration Committee and the Audit Committee. He has held Non-Executive Director posts in many companies and has been Chairman of several, including JPM European Smaller Companies Investment Trust Plc, Aon UK Limited and Bridgewell Group Plc. Prior to that, he was European CEO of Deutsche Asset Management from 2002 to 2005, global CEO of Rothschild Asset Management from 1999 to 2002, and founding CEO of Threadneedle Asset Management Limited from 1994 to 1999, when he was also a Director of Eagle Star and Allied Dunbar.

Anna Manz – Diageo Plc

Anna is the Group Strategy Director of Diageo Plc and a member of Diageo's Executive Committee. Prior to this Anna held a number of senior finance positions in Diageo, most recently as Regional Finance Director for Asia Pacific based in Singapore and prior to that as Group Treasurer based in London. She was a Trustee of Diageo's UK Defined Benefit Pension fund. Anna has been with Diageo for 15 years, and prior to that held finance roles with ICI and Unilever. Anna graduated from Wadham College, Oxford, in 1995 with an MA in Chemistry.

Luis Maroto – Amadeus

Luis Maroto became President and CEO of Amadeus in January 2011. He had joined Amadeus in 1999 as Director of Marketing Finance, from which he was promoted to Chief Financial Officer and then Deputy CEO. He was instrumental in Amadeus's return to the stock market with the company's successful IPO in 2010. Prior to joining Amadeus, Luis held important management positions in Bertelsmann Group in the areas of marketing and business planning, and finance. A Spanish citizen, he graduated in Law from Madrid's Complutense University, later gaining an MBA from the IESE and further qualifications from Harvard Business School and Stanford.

James Meekings – Funding Circle

James is Chief Commercial Officer at Funding Circle, the world's leading online marketplace for business loans. James is responsible for commercial development, growth, and launching Funding Circle into new finance markets. Prior to Funding Circle, James was at OC&C Strategy Consultants, where he advised companies on strategy and growth. James has a first-class degree from Oxford in Economics and Management. Funding Circle is the UK's largest peer-to-peer business lender. Since 2010, Funding Circle has enabled thousands of British small businesses to borrow more than £400 million directly from investors.

Brian Newman – PepsiCo

Brian is a 22-year veteran of PepsiCo. He began his PepsiCo career in Corporate Strategy, and went on to work in Finance & Strategy leadership roles in North America, Europe, and Asia. He has spent time in Business Development in Europe and served as the Treasurer for The Pepsi Bottling Group. Brian has held Country CFO roles in Canada, Russia, and China. Most recently he led the Corporate Strategy function and also served as the CFO for the Global Groups at PepsiCo. He worked in Investment Banking prior to joining PepsiCo. Brian is currently the Global Head of e-Commerce for PepsiCo and is based in New York City.

Mark Newton-Jones – Mothercare

Mark Newton-Jones is the CEO of Mothercare Plc, the leading global retailer for parents and young children, operating in more than 60 countries worldwide. Previously, Mark was CEO of Shop Direct Group, a position he held for almost ten years. Under Mark's stewardship, Shop Direct embarked on one of the largest retail integrations in Europe and a significant transformation journey, from a failing large-scale bricks-and-mortar operation to one of the UK's leading multichannel retailers with seamlessly integrated mobile, online, and digital platforms. Previously, Mark spent 18 years at Next, rising to become the youngest regional manager, with responsibility for over 100 stores, at the age of 25. Mark began his retail career in his family-run retail and wholesale business, working alongside his father and grandfather.

Frederik Nieuwenhuys – Dutch e-commerce entrepreneur

Frederik Nieuwenhuys is a Dutch e-commerce entrepreneur and OC&C alumnus. Having worked for six years with OC&C, Frederik co-founded

Fredhopper, an e-commerce software company. Fredhopper is the inventor of the world's leading targeting software to optimize the shelves in online stores. Fredhopper's personalization technologies enable retailers to systematically improve targeting. After having sold Fredhopper successfully to SDL Plc in 2010, Nieuwenhuys and his former partner created Escalada, an investment firm focused on online retail.

Roger Parry CBE – YouGov

Roger Parry is Chairman of Aves Enterprises (intellectual property), MSQ Partners (marketing communications), Mobile Streams (mobile media), and YouGov (market research). Previously, he was CEO of More Group and Clear Channel International, Chairman of Johnston Press, Future Publishing, and Shakespeare's Globe, Deputy Chairman of Clear Media in China, and a Director of Aegis, Internet Indirect, iTouch, New Media Spark and WCRS. He started his career as a broadcaster with BBC and ITV and then as a consultant at McKinsey & Company. He was an owner of the radio stations LBC and Jazz FM. Roger was educated at the universities of Bristol and Oxford, where he is a Visiting Fellow. He was awarded a CBE for services to media. He is the author of five books, including *Ascent of Media*.

Gavin Patterson – BT Group Plc

Gavin Patterson was appointed Chief Executive of the global communications services company BT Group in September 2013. Gavin joined BT in 2004 and became a member of the board in 2008, holding several posts, including creating BT Sport, until he was promoted to Chief Executive. He previously spent four years at Telewest (now Virgin Media), where in March 2000 he launched broadband in the UK. Prior to this, he spent nine years at Procter and Gamble, rising to become European Marketing Director. From 2010–13 Gavin sat on the advisory board of the Cambridge Judge Business School and from 2011–14 he was President of the Advertising Association. In addition, Gavin is a Non-Executive Director of British Airways and a Trustee of The British Museum.

Elsa Pekmez Atan – Enpara

Elsa Pekmez Atan is an Executive Vice President in charge of Enpara.com, a direct-only bank owned by Finansbank, serving more than 315,000 customers as of June 2015. Prior to joining Finansbank in 2010, Elsa worked for McKinsey & Company for over ten years. She has an MBA from Harvard Business School and a BA in Business Administration from Bosphorus (Boğaziçi) University.

Richard Pennycook – the Co-operative Group

Richard has nearly 25 years' experience in retail, starting with the management buyout of Allders in the late 1980s, where he was the CFO of European Duty Free and ran the North American operation for a time. Over the years, he has been involved in the growth of JD Wetherspoon and the turnarounds of Morrisons, Laura Ashley, Welcome Break, and Bulmers. Previously a Non-Executive Director of Richer Sounds, Richard is now Non-Executive Chairman of The Hut Group and a Non-Executive Director at Howdens and Persimmon.

Robert Philpott – Harte Hanks

Robert Philpott is a career marketing executive and has held senior leadership roles in Europe, Asia and the Americas. He is currently Chief Executive Officer at Harte Hanks, a US public company specializing in direct marketing. Prior to this Mr Philpott was a member of the board of Directors of Aegis Group Plc, from 2010 through 2012, and Chief Executive Officer of Synovate, a global market research firm. He joined Synovate in 1997, and after progressing through several operating positions was appointed Chief Executive Officer in 2009; he left Synovate for Harte Hanks in 2011 after its sale to Ipsos SA.

Marcelo Picanço – Porto Seguro

Mr Picanço has since 2006 been the CFO and Investor Relations Officer at Porto Seguro, a leading Brazilian insurance company, where he also holds an executive position as Financial Services (credit cards, auto finance, investment funds) and Life & Pension Officer. Prior to that Mr Picanço was a management consultant at Booz Allen Hamilton, serving clients especially in the financial sector.

Peter Plumb – MoneySuperMarket.com

Peter Plumb is the Chief Executive Officer of MoneySuperMarket.com Group Plc, which he joined in 2008. Prior to this role he held senior commercial positions with dunnhumby, Disney, Dyson, and PepsiCo Foods Ltd. Mr Plumb has an MBA from IMD Business School in Switzerland and a BSc (Hons) Civil Engineering from the University of Birmingham.

Michael Polk – Newell Rubbermaid

Michael Polk has been President and Chief Executive Officer since July 2011 and a member of the Board of Directors of Newell Rubbermaid since 2009. Previously, Mike was President of Global Foods, Home and Personal Care at Unilever, where he was responsible for the development, innovation, and marketing of Unilever's entire $64-billion portfolio of categories and brands. During eight years at Unilever, he is credited with transforming the company's business in the Americas, sharpening Unilever's global portfolio strategy, and creating a more competitive, faster-growing, innovation-driven organization. He was a member of the Unilever Executive Board from 2007–11. Earlier, Mike spent 16 years at Kraft Foods, culminating in serving as President, Asia Pacific Region, Kraft Foods International.

Spencer Rascoff – Zillow

Spencer Rascoff is CEO of Zillow Group, having joined in 2005 and served in various roles until his appointment to CEO in 2010, since when he has led Zillow through its IPO and nine acquisitions. His first book, the co-written *Zillow Talk: The New Rules of Real Estate*, is a *New York Times* bestseller. Fortune and Forbes both listed Spencer as one of America's most powerful CEOs under 40, and he is a recipient of Ernst & Young's National Entrepreneur of the Year Award. Before joining Zillow, Spencer was Vice President of Lodging for Expedia. In 1999, at the age of 24, Spencer co-founded Hotwire.com, a leading Internet travel company, which he then sold to InterActiveCorp (the parent company of Expedia). Spencer is on the boards of companies including TripAdvisor and Zulily, is a member of the Young Presidents' Organization, and is on the advisory board of Seattle Children's Hospital Research Institute.

John Roberts – AO

John Roberts is a founding Director who established the business AO World Plc in 2000. Since co-founding the group, John has presided over the evolution of the business and led the management team, which has successfully developed and expanded the group's business during periods of challenging market conditions, with a limited capital base. John ranked second in the 2013 *Sunday Times* Best Companies Best Leader category and ranked at number seven in *Management Today*'s Top 100 Entrepreneurs 2014. He is from Bolton and is a passionate supporter of staff participation in local charitable causes.

Sidar Sahin – Peak Games

Sidar founded Peak Games, one of the fastest-growing online and mobile gaming companies globally. Before founding Peak Games in 2010, Sidar co-founded Trendyol, one of the biggest e-commerce companies in Turkey, where he helped the venture grow from three to 300 people and reach a $100 million valuation within a year. His previous ventures include Funpac, a mobile gaming studio which he set up in 2002, Izlesene.com, a venture focused on social video sharing launched in early 2006, which was the highest-value Internet business exit in Turkey at the time. Sidar has a passion and talent for growing businesses and teams to their greatest potential.

Antoine de Saint-Affrique – Unilever

Antoine de Saint-Affrique was appointed President of Unilever's Food category in September 2011. Unilever Foods is a $15 billion business, with worldwide presence through iconic brands such as Knorr and Hellmann's. Prior to this, Antoine was Executive Vice President of Unilever's Skin category, and previously he was based in Moscow as Executive Vice President for Unilever's Central and Eastern Europe region – an area covering 21 countries. Antoine has a degree from ESSEC in Paris, and a qualification in Executive Education from Harvard Business School. Since 2004, he has led the marketing course at Mines ParisTech. A French national, Antoine has lived in Africa, the US, Hungary, the Netherlands, and Russia and is now based in the UK. He serves as a Non-Executive

Director at Essilor International, and has been Conseiller du Commerce Extérieur de la France since 2004.

Marjorie Scardino – The MacArthur Foundation

Marjorie Scardino was for 12 years Chief Executive (first in America and then worldwide) of *The Economist* and then in 1997 became the Chief Executive of Pearson Plc, the world's leading education company and the owner of Penguin Books and The Financial Times Group. She retired from that position in January 2013, and is currently the Chairman of The MacArthur Foundation. MacArthur is one of the world's largest independent foundations, working on a wide-ranging program, from community and economic development to digital learning, juvenile justice, international human rights, peace and security, and environmental conservation. She is also the Chairman-elect of the London School for Hygiene and Tropical Medicine, a member of the non-profit boards of Oxfam, The Royal College of Art, and The Carter Center, as well as the for-profit boards of Twitter and IAG (the holding company of British Airways, Iberia, and other airlines). Dame Marjorie was raised in Texas, trained as a lawyer, practiced in Georgia for a decade and began there, with her husband, the Pulitzer Prize-winning *Georgia Gazette* newspaper. She has received a number of honorary degrees, and in 2003 was dubbed a Dame of the British Empire. She is also a member of the Royal Society of the Arts in the UK and the American Association of Arts and Sciences.

Cassius Schymura – Santander

Mr Schymura is the Director of Cards and Personal Banking Products at Santander, where he has worked since 2004. He started his career in Financial Services at Unibanco (currently Itaú-Unibanco) back in 1989. After that, he served at Booz & Company as a Senior Associate, and assumed executive positions at Ideias Net and Softcorp.

Tom Seery – RealSelf

Tom Seery is the Founder and CEO of RealSelf, a Seattle-based startup that brings transparency to the multi-billion-dollar cosmetic medicine and aesthetics industry. Over the past eight years Tom has nurtured

RealSelf into a vibrant community that shares deep, personal experiences associated with cosmetic surgery, reconstructive surgery, dermatology, bariatrics, and dentistry. Prior to RealSelf, Tom worked at Expedia, Unisys Corporation, and had a stint in Washington DC, acting as handler for a US Congressman. He holds an MS from Drexel University, an MBA from the University of Washington, and a BA from Connecticut College. When not working on RealSelf or chasing his two toddlers, Tom is passionate about international adoption, bringing reconstructive surgery to the poor in developing countries, and growing tomatoes that ripen before the sun disappears.

S. Sivakumar – ITC Agribusiness

Mr Sivakumar is the Group Head of Agri and IT Businesses of ITC Limited, itcportal.com. He runs a billion-dollar agribusiness, is the Vice Chairman of ITC Infotech – a global IT services company – and the Chairman of Technico, an agri-biotech company. Mr Sivakumar is well known as the architect of the world-famous farmer empowerment initiative, ITC e-Choupal, which benefits over 4 million farmers through customized agri-extension and market linkage services, while providing a unique source of competitive advantage to ITC's packaged foods business. Mr Sivakumar is Chairman of the National Agricultural Council of the Confederation of Indian Industry (CII), Vice Chairman of the World Economic Forum's Global Agenda Council on Social Innovation, and a member of the UN Global Compact's Core Advisory Group to develop Sustainable Agriculture Business Principles.

Artur Smolarek – PZU Group

Artur Smolarek has fifteen years of management consulting experience and spent over six years at top executive positions in the financial services and healthcare sectors. As a Principal at the Boston Consulting Group, Artur has worked mainly for financial services and FMCG companies on growth and commercial strategies, and restructuring cases, as well as M&A and post-merger integrations. He also held a CFO position in one of the leading Polish Banks. For the past five years Artur has been Managing Director, Health Insurance Division, at PZU Group, Poland, one of the largest insurance groups in the CEE Region.

Sir Martin Sorrell – WPP

Sir Martin Sorrell founded WPP, the world's leading advertising and marketing services group, in 1985 and has been Chief Executive throughout. Collectively, WPP employs over 179,000 people (including associates) in over 3,000 offices in 111 countries. Sir Martin actively supports the advancement of international business schools – advising Harvard, IESE, the Indian School of Business, the China Europe International Business School, and Fundação Dom Cabral Business School in Brazil. He has been publicly recognized with a number of awards, including the Harvard Business School Alumni Achievement Award. In the *Time* "100 Builders & Titans" he was voted one of the world's most influential figures in business. He received a knighthood in January 2000. He is on the Executive Committee of the World Economic Forum International Business Council (having been Chairman from 2010–12) and a member of the Business Council in the US.

Kurt Staelens – Macintosh

Kurt Staelens was appointed as a member of the Managing Board and CEO of Macintosh in July 2014. Mr Staelens has Belgian nationality. He was previously Vice-President of Sales and E-Business at telecoms company Belgacom in Brussels, a position he held from 2012 to 2014. In the course of his career he has held various commercial management positions and also owned his own online business. Mr Staelens is Belgian and studied at KU Leuven and graduated with distinction in 1991, having obtained a Masters degree (MSc) in Commercial Engineering. In 1996 he was awarded an MBA by the Kellogg School of Management, Northwestern University, USA, graduating with high distinction.

Tim Steiner – Ocado

Tim is a founding Director of Ocado, the largest online food retailer in the world. He has responsibility for keeping a general oversight of the business and strategy. Prior to Ocado, Tim spent eight years as a banker at Goldman Sachs. During his time there, he was based in London, Hong Kong and New York in the Fixed Income division. Tim graduated from Manchester University with an honours degree in Economics, Finance, and Accountancy in 1992. Ocado has been voted the best online supermarket in the UK by *Which?* every year since 2010.

Andy Street – John Lewis

Andy has spent his career at the John Lewis Partnership, joining after graduating from Oxford with a degree in Politics, Philosophy, and Economics in 1985. Andy became Managing Director of the John Lewis Division in 2007 and has led the business through times of significant change in both the economy and the retail industry at large. During this time, John Lewis's gross sales have increased by 35% to over £4 billion, it has opened 16 new shops, and the department store has become one of the UK's most respected and successful retailers. Andy is Chair of the Greater Birmingham and Solihull Local Enterprise Partnership (LEP), and he is a member of the Prime Minister's Business Advisory Group.

Rogério Takayanagi – TIM Fiber

Mr Takayanagi has been the CEO of TIM Fiber since its start up in 2011. Prior to that, he was CMO at TIM, co-leading the turnaround process of a major mobile operator in Brazil, and was also the CEO of Intelig, a long-distance carrier. Before embracing executive positions in telecom companies, Mr Takayanagi was a management consultant at Spectrum, Value Partners, and Promon.

Prashant Tandon – HealthKart.com

Prashant is the Managing Director and Co-Founder of HealthKart.com, India's premium e-health store. Previously Prashant worked at McKinsey & Company in San Francisco, advising Fortune healthcare companies, and prior to that he was part of the business leadership program at Hindustan Unilever Limited, where he managed development for one of the largest brands across Asia (Lux, across 13 countries). Prashant launched the GPS navigation product line of MapMyIndia in 2007 in the Indian market. He holds a Bachelor of Technology from IIT Delhi and is a graduate of Stanford Business School.

Anne Tse – PepsiCo

Anne Tse is the General Manager, New Business, of PepsiCo. The New Business team is PepsiCo's growth engine for China Foods, in terms of topline growth, innovation pipelines, and new ways of working. Prior to this, Anne was the Head of Strategy for PepsiCo Greater China Region. Before joining PepsiCo, Anne was an Associate Partner at McKinsey & Company, focusing in Greater China Consumer Practice; and subsequently, CEO of Mannings China, a subsidiary of Dairy Farm International, the largest Asia-based retailer. Anne grew up in Hong Kong and obtained her MBA from the Kellogg School of Management, Northwestern University.

John Walden – Home Retail Group

John joined Argos as Managing Director in 2012 and was promoted to Group CEO in 2014. He started his retail career in the 1990s as Chief Operating Officer of Peapod, a pioneer in online supermarket retailing. He joined Best Buy, the giant US electricals retailer, in 1999, as President of its Internet and direct channels division, and over an eight-year career also served as Executive Vice President, Human Capital, and Leadership, and ultimately as Executive Vice President of its Customer Business Group. John later moved to Sears, where he served as Chief Customer Officer and Executive Vice President. Additionally he was appointed President and CEO of Inversion Inc., a retail consultancy, and Chief Executive of Activeion Cleaning Solutions.

Mike Walsh – LexisNexis

Mike Walsh is CEO of the global legal business of LexisNexis, a leading provider of information solutions to law firm, corporate, government, and academic markets. The business serves customers in over 175 countries and employs 10,000 people worldwide. Prior to his current role, Mr Walsh was CEO of LexisNexis US Legal Markets. He led the transformation of the business from a provider of legal research to a solutions partner. Mr Walsh joined LexisNexis in 2003 as Senior Vice President, Global Strategy and Business Development, where he helped oversee significant expansion into the LexisNexis Risk Management sector. Prior to joining LexisNexis, Mr Walsh was Director of Strategic Business Development at Home Depot.

Christian Wegner – ProSiebenSat.1

Dr Christian Wegner joined ProSiebenSat.1 in 2004 and was appointed a member of the Executive Board in 2011, having held several management positions. Previously Dr Wegner was a member of the management team at SevenOne Media GmbH. As Chief Integration Officer at ProSiebenSat.1 he oversaw the merger process between ProSiebenSat.1 and SBS. Before that he worked for five years as a consultant at McKinsey & Company, supporting clients in the media, private equity, and financial sectors. Dr Christian Wegner studied Business Administration in Frankfurt am Main and took his PhD at Witten-Herdecke University and the Schloss Reichartshausen European Business School.

Stefan Winners – Burda

Stefan Winners is a member of the Management Board of the Hubert Burda Media Group and is Chair of the Supervisory Board of Tomorrow Focus AG, which he previously served as CEO. He is also Chair of the supervisory board of XING AG and a member of the supervisory boards of zooplus AG and Giesecke & Devrient. Prior to this, he held various management positions at Vogel Business Medien GmbH & Co KG in Würzburg, and awk Außenwerbung in Koblenz, as well as at the Bertelsmann Group company Heinze GmbH. Stefan Winners graduated in Business Administration at the University of Passau in Germany and completed the Advanced Management Program (AMP) at Harvard Business School.

Gang Yu – Yihaodian

Gang Yu is the Co-Founder and Chairman of Yihaodian, yhd.com, a leading e-commerce company in China with over 80 million customers. Prior to founding Yihaodian, he was Vice President, Worldwide Procurement at Dell Inc. Dr Yu also served as Vice President, Worldwide Supply Chain Operations at Amazon.com. Before Amazon, Dr Yu served as the Jack G. Taylor Chair Professor in Business at the University of Texas, Austin, Director of the Center for Management of Operations and Logistics, and co-Director of the Center for Decision Making Under Uncertainty. Dr Yu has also received numerous international awards, published over 80 journal articles as well as four books, and holds three US patents.

Index

Printed and bound by CPI Group (UK) Ltd, Croydon, CR0 4YY